HOW**WHY**
WOMEN
CAN**NEED**
CH**ELP**ANGE

Sophie Gallagher

HOW WHY WOMEN MEN CANEED CHELPE

A GUIDE TO UNDOING HARM AND BEING A BETTER ALLY

WELBECK

Published by Welbeck
An imprint of Welbeck Non-Fiction Limited,
part of Welbeck Publishing Group.
Based in London and Sydney
www.welbeckpublishing.com

First published by Welbeck in 2022

A CIP catalogue record for this book is available from the British Library

ISBN
Hardback – 9781802792973
eBook – 9781802792980

Typeset by seagulls.net
Printed and bound in the UK

10 9 8 7 6 5 4 3 2 1

Every reasonable effort has been made to trace copyright holders of
material produced in this book, but if any have been inadvertently
overlooked the publishers would be glad to hear from them.

For my mum, Angela

Contents

Contents

Trigger warning: There will be extensive discussion of men's violence against women in this book. For those who are looking for support, please find a list of organisations at the back (see Useful Resources, pages 211–28).

Introduction

It was a school night and we should have been in bed, and asleep, hours ago. On our way back from a gig, my friend and I had been dropped at the bus station in the middle of town and from there decided to walk the quickest route home – rather than the busiest or best-lit – to make up for the lost time. Two 17-year-old girls pacing alongside the suburban Essex bypass, a steady stream of cars driving by.

A lone man came into view on the path ahead. Standing in the centre of the pavement he was moving slowly towards us. Objectively, nothing had yet happened to indicate we should be scared – and of course we outnumbered him two to one – but my stomach lurched all the same. The only other routes available at this point were to turn back to where we'd come from, moving further away from the safety of our beds and still with no guarantee of security, to divert into a dark and totally empty park or to keep walking straight ahead. We quickened the pace, walking onwards, clasping our hands together.

No longer on the horizon, the man was now only a couple of feet away, eyes fixed on us. My mind raced through the numerous ways we could have avoided being in this situation: a different route, an earlier time, not going out at all. He said and did nothing as we passed – less than a metre apart – but as we glanced back, he was no longer walking in the opposite direction but had turned and was following us. Our unspoken fear felt realised: we ran.

This is not a remarkable story. It is painfully commonplace, taken from an encyclopaedic bank of stories that will ring familiar to women and girls, of all ages, across the UK. It ended when we, breathlessly, reached a nearby fish and chip shop that was mercifully open and occupied by a handful of people. Although there was no physical violence in this encounter, the underlying threat that we felt in those two minutes offers a snapshot into women's everyday fear of men's potential for violence. It shows the way that this fear can restrict our freedom to claim space in the world and the constant work to keep ourselves safe or the self-policing we undertake in a bid to mitigate the risk, despite knowing it is ultimately futile if a man really wishes to do us harm.

In the last few years, newspaper headlines, TV bulletins, radio broadcasts and conversations on social media have been dominated by high-profile examples of violence against women. Countless numbers of supposedly watershed moments and the media circus that ensues. The murders of Sabina Nessa, Ashling Murphy, Sarah Everard, Gabby Petito, Bibaa Henry, Nicole Smallman, Joy Morgan, Libby Squire, Grace Millane, and the many other women who got nowhere near the same level of column inches or attention. There has also been a widely documented rise in reports of drink spiking at nightclubs and the launch of campaigns like Soma Sara's Everyone's Invited, exposing rape culture in schools and higher education. The Covid-19 lockdown saw domestic abuse spiral to record highs with helplines like Refuge reporting a 60 per cent rise in the number of monthly contacts in what was described as a 'shadow pandemic'. Women's Aid reported that at one point in lockdown they had a queue of 21,000 users trying to access their live chat support. Even attempts by women to demonstrate solidarity and grief, like the Clapham Common vigil for Sarah Everard in March 2021, resulted in state violence.

Although these instances of violence are shocking – dashcam footage, court documents and CCTV stills of final bus journeys or supermarket trips, bringing the full horror of a woman's last minutes into vivid and gruesome clarity – they are not surprising for women. Women are taught to live with a constant humming fear of men, an instinctive reflex, one that waxes and wanes on any given day, minute, moment. This does not mean they cower in sight of any and all men, but learn early that this is seen as a man's world, we're just living in it. To enter into public space is to do so at a potential cost to yourself, an eternal risk assessment. Of course, women know that not all men present a danger, but we can also never be sure which ones do.

In writing this book, I found it hard, almost impossible at times, to articulate the pervasiveness of this. For women, living with this knowledge is both excruciatingly conscious and at the same time so ingrained as to be invisible. It sits deep within me. It is self-preservation. It is the reason I have never walked alone through a park after dark, I sit near other women on the train if possible and I always know who is walking behind me. It is omnipresent.

Gender-based violence might be perceived as extreme – of course the consequences and harms are so – but seeing this violence only through a lens of extremity does a disservice to those it harms. It is not a lone force moving on the outskirts of society, it is the natural conclusion, a byproduct, of the patriarchal system and inequality we live under. The use of violence may feel disconnected from the everyday for many men, but it is made possible by a shared system that has preserved men's dominance and women's inferiority, held up by our history, our culture, our values, our media and our economic systems. In a society that still has a gender pay gap, is content with women doing millions of hours of unpaid labour each year, does not have an equal representation of women in politics, on screen, or in boardrooms, laughs at rape jokes and only recently removed topless women from the pages of national newspapers, is it any wonder we're still struggling with violence fuelled by male entitlement and power? Because patriarchal violence is not just about individual men, it is a sign of a sprawling web of control that normalises and trivialises women being harmed.

There can be phenomenal reluctance to connect sexism and sexual violence with women's lower economic, social and cultural standing, but this sub-status is implicitly linked. Because when society sees women's needs, their wants, their ambitions, their intelligence, their capability, their leadership as secondary to men, one in which women are dehumanised, it creates the conditions for men to use control if it further serves their needs.

We have to get better at connecting the dots between the sexist comments made in the pub, the presumption that women will always give up their careers for children, the leering at a girl in her school uniform, the not taking women seriously and the dispensation of violence. All of these systemic issues are on the same spectrum of inequality. Holding prejudiced attitudes about the role of women, whether in the bedroom, the office or the kitchen, moves women from being on par with men to second-class citizens. If men are taught that they are worth more, that they are smarter, their voice should be louder, their opinions more valid, their sexual needs more pressing, then dishing out violence for their own goals is put within reach. It is appeased and tolerated. Even by those men who do not necessarily believe themselves to hold such gender bias or see women any differently than men. Even by those men who are upset by the persistent violence they read about. It makes all men complicit.

When we are looking at the news, asking how yet another woman has died at the hands of a man, we have to join all the bits of the puzzle together. To look at the big picture rather than seeing the violence as a problem that is independent of everything else. As civil rights leader Martin Luther King Jr wrote in his open letter from a Birmingham jail in April 1963: 'I am sure that none of you would want to rest content with the superficial kind of social analysis that deals merely with effects and does not grapple with underlying causes.' We must assess how men and women are told to move about in the world long before the first punch is thrown. This means bringing in men who do not use violence but benefit from, and perpetuate, the same systems of inequality that prop up those who do use violence. To see that the absence of bad behaviour does not make one's behaviour good *enough*. To ask what men are proactively doing to combat the issue. Men's allyship cannot be assumed, it is acquired through action.

Moments of learning and collective consciousness-raising sometimes come like a dripping tap, reaching a critical mass before spilling over. Others hit like a tidal wave. Building on the historic #MeToo movement (started by activist Tarana Burke on MySpace in 2006 and reaching global fame in 2017 in the wake of accusations against former Hollywood producer Harvey Weinstein), every new frontpage tragedy paints a picture in the public mind of what violence against women is, how it happens and how often. But the image it depicts is often an incomplete one. Not only do we give more airtime to the stories of some women (the white and middle class rather than, say, women of colour); but violence is reported on without setting it in the context of wider misogyny; we favour the most headline-grabbing examples over the daily inequalities that form the backdrop to women's lives and we almost universally omit the role of the perpetrators – men.

One might naively assume that the national conversation following the deaths of women at the hands of men would go something like this: 'Men, stop being violent towards women!' But that couldn't be further from the truth. Men's violence is instead still seen as a women's issue and as such, something for women to resolve alone. Consider the days after Sarah Everard's murder by police officer Wayne Couzens. Women were told, among many other things, that in future if they felt unsafe they should flag down a bus, run to a nearby house, be more legally savvy and even resist arrest. Although Philip Allott, the North Yorkshire Police, Fire and Crime commissioner who made some of these comments, resigned, his comments – and those of others, who remained in their jobs – are a symptom of a system rather than the cause. In 2018, after a string of sexual assaults near Willesden Green tube station, women were told to stop wearing their headphones or using handheld devices at night. In March 2021, a former Met detective, Sue Hill, appeared on ITV's *This Morning* to tell an audience eating their cornflakes that women should '[wear] shoes that you can run away [in] if need be' and 'keep looking over your shoulder' when walking home. After the September 2021 killing of primary-school teacher Sabina Nessa in Kidbrooke, south-east London, while she was on a short walk to meet a friend for a Friday-night drink, women were handed heart-shaped rape alarms and informed on leaflets distributed locally that they should 'look assertive and walk with confidence' when they leave home. That particular advice page on the Met

Police website has now been deleted but the piecemeal policies continue – BT chipped in with a suggested 888 hotline women could ring to track them on their way home.

Not only do some suggestions seem wide open to abuse (software that tracks women's movements, come on!), where are the questions about what men should be doing? About how they could help? Why do we allocate no role for men to end men's violence? Why is men's violence a women's issue? Why do we so readily accept that violent men have the right to exist and women just have to find innovative ways to work around them? Why not address the root cause of the problem rather than sticking plasters on the consequences?

If this line of questioning has already made you baulk, do not walk away. This book will be unapologetic in naming the gendered problem of men's violence against women – you cannot hope to fix a problem without naming it – but equally, it does not tar all men with a violent brush. Of course, it is not the case that all men are committing grievous acts of violence, but it is time we face up to the gaping hole in our conversation and confront the falsehood that the perpetrators are aberrations or outsiders. The existence of violence as a disproportionate and gendered harm is not up for debate and its intrinsic ties to other inequalities remains fundamentally overlooked. Accepting this as fact does not make women or men 'anti-men', it simply recognises the reality of what we all face. And seeing oneself as an innocent man is not enough to ignore the problem: all men must feel compelled to act.

How Men Can Help has two overarching messages. It brings together strands that are often seen as disparate – women's inequality across society and men's violence towards women – and wants to start a frank conversation about why men are largely left out of the solution. Handing the issue to women to both suffer under and solve for themselves. In doing so, it gives men the tools and the moment to change, to do more and do better. Consider this book both the motivation and the guidance you need to make those long-harboured aspirations a reality.

I have covered this topic as a journalist for more than half a decade now. A turning point in my understanding of violence against women came in 2017 when I was travelling home on the London Underground from work and was sent 120 images of an erect penis over Apple's AirDrop (Bluetooth) function. They had been sent by someone in my carriage – the AirDrop range was only 6m (20ft) – but the sender was anonymous. I was not only embarrassed and furious at the invasion of my space but scared that the perpetrator might escalate the behaviour, follow me off the train or harass me in person. I reported it to the police but, after some initial promising noises, the case fizzled. I have since spoken with over 90 women who also experienced cyber flashing. Most had not reported it, in part because the most common response they'd had from people was asking why they had AirDrop turned on at all. Instead of blaming men, we are generally more comfortable either disbelieving women or implying that they must somehow have been at fault (AirDrop turned on) and so invited the harm. You might have heard this described as 'victim-blaming', but it is more explicitly women-blaming.

Even though cyber flashing is a relatively new crime, it became clear to me at that point that we are already modelling the same responses and treatment that we always have done when it comes to gendered violence. That women should have done more, been smarter, used more common sense, while largely abdicating men – both perpetrators and others – of any accountability or requirement to stop. The focus has always been, and seems will always be, on how women will prevent it, on better ways for women to police men's behaviour when it is happening or about to happen, to reduce their chances of victimhood and by implication send the perpetrator elsewhere, to another woman (or simply you at a later time or date when your guard is down). But that is about to change.

This book is for those men who want to be part of that change, men who are ready to listen to women, stand alongside them and share in the responsibility of tackling the problem. Perhaps you sought this book out in a bid to start a journey or someone bought it for you, passed it along as an act of kindness, feeling you might find its contents useful. It will focus on the UK experience as that is my region of expertise, with some references to organisations like White Ribbon or MenEngage that work across the globe. Across 13 chapters, it aims to get men to see how stepping up to the plate is not just in the interests of the women they know and love (we should avoid only eliciting men's compassion based on proximity, i.e. fear about what might happen to their wife, daughter, sister), but as a broader social justice issue that we must all fix. Doing this work will also, crucially, benefit men.

Feminist Gloria Steinem said in 2019: 'I think it's helpful to realise men's stake in it. Because actually if you look at the cause of male deaths, speeding and violence, and you add them all up, the [advancement of] the women's movement and dissolution of gender roles means that [men] would have about five more years of life to live. This is not bad. Who else can make that offer?' Although Steinem was half-joking, she struck a crucial point: 'Tell them the masculine realm is killing them,' she said. Both men and women are happier in more gender equal societies (the Nordic countries measure highly on such scores). Founder of the Women's Equality Party, Sophie Walker, told me: 'If you look at the data around the world, the countries that are closest to [equality] show that both men and women are happiest. It's not just that the economies are working better. It's that mental health rates are better, divorce rates are lower. The biggest lie of all is that men are flourishing [now]. There's a very small handful of very powerful men who enjoy that power.' There will be personal benefits for men – breaking away from parts of masculinity that are damaging, closer relationships with women, reducing the friendly fire of male-on-male violence – but also more flexible divisions of labour, a greater pool of talent for workplaces and improvements for the economy.*

---

* Research by the House of Commons has found companies with more female leaders outperform those dominated by men, 2022.

When I started my research for *How Men Can Help* I was surprised by how much of the literature on the role of men in solution-building is written by men for men; perhaps that is testament to how few men read books by women (women are 65 per cent more likely to read non-fiction by the opposite sex than men are) or how infrequently men wish themselves to be put under the microscope by women. One of the smartest moves in the so-called men's rights movement, which now finds a home and many welcoming ears on the internet, has been to frame any attempts to do so as inherently at the expense of men. A study from 2020 found 50 per cent of men thought feminism had gone too far.*

Indeed, some might feel frustrated I have not yet mentioned the violence men face. While it is somewhat understandable that some see this omission and feel drawn to blaming women as an explanation, it is a diversion and a con. It is a strategic bid to build resistance and wants to stop men asking – what if doing this work could benefit us all? What if the very issues – that you feel women ignore – like violence against men or men's high suicide rates are in fact a product of the same system? But it is useful to do a little expectation management. *How Men Can Help* will not

---

* Dr Fiona Vera-Gray, author of *The Right Amount of Panic: How Women Trade Freedom*, says: 'We're seeing a form of radicalisation of young men that is specifically anti-feminist. We're starting to see that translate into students in their first year of university, saying there is no gender pay gap, women lie about rape.'

be a sugar-coated tick list of ways men can do the bare minimum, earn a 'good man' badge, graduate at the back of these pages and forget about it. It will not be an issue men can babysit for a short period – gaining praise in the process – before handing it back to women. In picking up this book you have taken the first step, but this work will not be achieved overnight. We need radical change. The effort that one man makes today or tomorrow could be enough to move the dial in his personal life, yet he is unlikely to individually overhaul society. Men, and women, should not find this to be a source of disillusionment when rallying behind this cause, but a source of hope for a future we will not live to see. We are the instigators of a gender revolution that will outlive us. A legacy that, done right, will liberate half of the population.

Women do not need men to be knights in shining armour riding in to save them, but for everyone to see how society allows men to ignore the problem of men's violence and why this now has to change. Each chapter title in this book will give you a step to take, touching on rejecting the #NotAllMen narrative, getting to grips with history, rethinking the gender pay gap, examining masculinity, rethinking consent and being okay with not having all the answers. Using personal stories, data and commentary, it is spread over three parts: accepting the reality of the situation in front of us and placing ourselves in the picture; understanding the wider social contexts that help normalise violence; and then the third part is more practical, a look ahead to changing our mindsets and, in time, our behaviour.

A word on language: in a topic that is so clearly gendered, it is important to give clarity around the use of certain terminology. For starters, although the word 'women' will be used for brevity, this is intended to include all those who identify as women. Non-binary and trans women are also subject to high levels of violence at the hands of men. Second, the phrase 'violence against women and girls' (referred to by the acronym VAWG) will be used throughout because it is commonplace in this field, particularly in policymaking. The UK government says it adopted it from the United Nations 1993 Declaration on the Elimination of Violence Against Women (DEVAW) and it does a good job of centring survivors and their voices, which is crucial. But it also does a fairly convenient job of removing men from the equation. It launders men's violence to become a violence that exists without anyone owning it or being responsible – it just seems to happen to women as they go about their day. As we will explore in this book, that removal of men often doesn't do us any favours.

The feminist movement and the relentless work of women has changed the landscape of this discussion, both in my lifetime and my career. These individuals and collectives have forced issues onto the agenda, given space and been unflinching in shining a light on the gendered persecution women face on a daily basis, as well as the intersectional layers of oppression that women of colour, disabled women, queer women, trans women and others deal with. Not to mention working on the frontlines on shoestring (and ever-dwindling) budgets. This book will never understate the importance of women's self-determination or their leadership and phenomenal expertise in this field, but acknowledge that it is time men felt accountable for their role in both the issue and the solution. It can no longer be considered *women's work* – men must step up and speak out now, too.

Accept Violence Against Women Happens – Even If You Don't See It

Every woman has heard the one about the ponytail. They won't necessarily know when they first heard it, who imparted the wisdom or which teenage magazine it was featured in, but they will have heard that wearing your hair tied up, rather than hanging down your back, apparently makes you easier to forcibly grab from behind. So, best to consider that nugget of wisdom when getting dressed. And remember to hold your keys between your fingers to use as a weapon when walking alone at night. To keep your headphones in to look like you are busy, but keep your music off so you can stay alert. Keep your phone within reach but do not let a conversation with a friend distract you. Keep an eye on your drink but don't seem too uptight. Be assertive but don't look a man straight in the eye. Go in pairs. Take a taxi. Don't be alone in a car with a man. Be polite to men. Laugh at their jokes. Don't lead them on. Take out shoes you can run in.

Walk down the middle of the road to avoid concealed alleyways or gaps in hedgerows. Shout 'Fire!', not 'Rape!' because help will come quicker. Plan your route before you leave the house, using only roads with street lights. Text when you get home.

Women make near-constant calculations about their safety. This isn't because they love doing this 'safety work' – a term coined by researchers Dr Fiona Vera-Gray and Professor Liz Kelly – or that they are unjustly and disproportionately paranoid. This is the product of years of conditioning from childhood, witnessing the regularity of men's violence around them and the playbook response, in the news, in popular culture and even from parents and caregivers (this includes women) that those who are hurt should have better protected themselves. This judgement can be explicit as well as unspoken. For months after Sabina Nessa's death if you googled her name the second suggested question under 'People Also Ask' was '*What was Sabina Nessa wearing?*' It now appears to have been removed. As well as this type of question, even well-intentioned quick fixes like tracking apps, street lighting or CCTV help codify the belief that it is only by adapting and safeguarding women's behaviour that we can bring an end to this problem. This is wrong, our whole approach needs to be flipped on its head.

First, let's take a step back and make sure we're all on the same page by crunching some numbers. In the UK a woman is killed every three days by a man. The Femicide Census, an organisation which collects information on women killed by men, calculates that 1,425 women were killed by men from 2009 to 2018 in Britain. Numbers are lower in late summer and autumn and nearly half (47 per cent) of all December femicides were over the Christmas and New Year period. Since 2009, there have been eight women killed on Christmas Day, five on Christmas Eve, five on New Year's Eve, three on Boxing Day and 12 on New Year's Day. Of these women, 62 per cent were killed by a current or former partner, which is by far the most common perpetrator-victim relationship when assessing femicides.

From April 2020 to March 2021 alone, 177 women were murdered in England and Wales, reports the Office for National Statistics (ONS). This was the same number as the year prior and lower than 2018–19 when it was 241 – the highest in a decade. Of course, men are also killed in large numbers, estimated to be an average of 399 male victims per year over the last decade, but the common denominator in the killing of both men and women is male perpetrators – a 2016 study from the University of Gothenburg in Sweden looked at 20 years of data from 1990–2010 and found that nine out of every 10 killers (90 per cent) were men. BBC analysis of UK data showed around 85 per cent of people sentenced in court for violent crimes were men.

The Crime Survey for England and Wales (2017) estimated 20 per cent of women, one in every five, have experienced some type of sexual assault or rape since the age of 16. This is equivalent to 3.4 million women. But 98.3 per cent of rapists, of both men and women, are men. Domestic abuse impacts 1.6 million women a year. Disabled women are twice as likely to experience domestic violence than non-disabled women (women's different types of identity, like race or sexuality, can interact in a way that creates distinct forms of violence). Again, 92 per cent of domestic abuse defendants in the year to March 2020 were men.

The statistics not only make clear that women suffer extensive levels of violence but that men are almost always the cause. Australian sociologist and co-editor of the *International Encyclopedia of Men and Masculinities*, Michael Flood, explains this succinctly: 'Most men don't use violence against women. But when violence [against women] occurs, it's largely by men.' Even when it comes to violence against men, the victims are still suffering at the hands of men. When we understand this, it seems incredibly disingenuous to suggest that women who want to stop men's violence are anti-men.

In July 2021, in a report by Her Majesty's Inspectorate of Constabulary, Zoë Billingham described the current situation as a 'national epidemic of violence' against women and girls. In recent years, Labour MP Jess Phillips has started a devastating but important parliamentary tradition on International Women's Day of reading out the names of the hundreds of women killed in the previous year. But if you look further you will see that official statistics are only the tip of the iceberg. The latest Crime Survey for England and Wales showed that fewer than one in six victims (16 per cent) had actually reported their assault to the police. This figure is consistent with the survey from three years prior (the interval at which they are conducted) in 2014, when it was 17 per cent. As if those numbers weren't low enough, some women face additional barriers to reporting.

Black and minoritised women can fear a racist response or disproportionate policing and sentencing for non-white perpetrators. A report by the University of Warwick and Imkaan, an organisation addressing violence against Black and minoritised women, says: 'Women's silence operates within and is maintained by a broader societal context of patriarchal control, which for minoritised women manifests in specific ways across diverse contexts.' Black women are 14 per cent less likely than white women to be referred to abuse support services by police when they do come forward. A woman's immigration status or language barriers might also stop her asking for help. Sex workers also face high rates of violence – studies estimate 70 to 80 per cent have been a victim – but this can go unreported, too.

Women all share an experience of oppression but not all women experience oppression in the same ways. Intersectionality is a term coined by Professor Kimberlé Crenshaw as a metaphor for understanding how multiple forms of inequality can compound themselves. It is a prism through which we can see how something isn't only a gender problem or a race problem: it can be both. These differences in reporting and low levels of women coming forward mean that while statistics give us a useful lens to examine the scale of men's violence, they cannot claim to capture the entire breadth and depth of the issue. They are only part of the jigsaw.

Even looking at cases charged by the police is no guarantee of an accurate portrayal. Dame Vera Baird QC, the Victims' Commissioner, said we have effectively 'decriminalised rape', when in 2019 the CPS only prosecuted 1,758 rape cases, a 52 per cent drop from two years before. It is abundantly clear that violence against women is not an imagined moral panic. Rather, the true scale of the problem is still largely obscured.

In addition to this criminal and deadly behaviour, women experience a full catalogue of misogyny and harassment, a lifetime of microaggressions, much more of which goes unreported and unremarked, forming the grinding backdrop to our daily lives. The harassment that becomes death by a thousand cuts.

A survey by the UN found over 70 per cent of women in the UK had experienced sexual harassment in public. This number rises to 97 per cent among 18–24-year-olds. A Plan International survey found the number was 88 per cent among mixed-race girls, 82 per cent of Black, African, Caribbean and Black British girls, and 70 per cent of Asian and Asian British girls. Over half of women had experienced catcalling, 40 per cent had been groped, a third had been followed and one in five had faced indecent exposure. Women, as a result, walk less in public than men. In almost every country in the world, they walk disproportionately fewer steps each day than men, according to a huge study by Stanford University. The study researcher said: 'If one person doesn't walk a whole lot, maybe they're lazy. If hundreds of thousands of people – and especially women – don't walk a lot? That's not an individual laziness problem, that's a societal problem.' Four out of five women (81 per cent) feel unsafe walking alone after dark in a park or other open space. And in the workplace, half of women (and two-thirds of 18–24-year-olds) have been victims of sexual harassment, most often inappropriate comments or touching, according to a joint 2016 YouGov and Trades Union Congress (TUC) survey.

Young girls are not exempt; a survey of 1,574 girls by Girlguiding in 2015 found that 81 per cent had experienced or witnessed sexism in the week before the survey. That is more than every eight in 10 young girls. A 2021 Ofsted rapid review, conducted in response to the volume of testimony on the *Everyone's Invited* website, found that sexual harassment was so normalised for young girls they saw no point in challenging or reporting it. The Everyday Sexism campaign, set up by Laura Bates in April 2012 to document women's experiences of sexism, received over 100,000 submissions in the first three years. Despite some optimism that lockdown might have improved this situation, by reducing the number of people out on the streets, this was not the case. A poll by Plan UK found a fifth of women experienced street harassment during the spring lockdown, a figure which rose to 51 per cent in summer as restrictions eased.

While the arrival of the internet has been a useful tool in allowing women to widely share examples of violence – particularly as we saw in the #MeToo movement, it has also allowed for the birth of online harms. These can include – but are not limited to, image-based abuse, cyber flashing, cyber stalking and trolling. One in five women in the UK has suffered online abuse, research by Amnesty uncovered. Almost half of those women said the abuse was sexist or mysogynistic and nearly a third threatened sexual or physical violence. This translates to real-world harms: 70 per cent of women who were subjected to this abuse reported low self-esteem as a result, 60 per cent had trouble sleeping and more than half suffered anxiety. There is also the harassment of high-profile women, particularly politicians. Black and Asian women MPs are abused at far greater levels, with Labour MP Diane Abbott alone receiving almost half of all abusive tweets sent to female MPs. For women these numbers might be shocking, but hardly surprising. Yet for men the message isn't always getting through.

In 2017, Eliza Hatch was walking down the street when a man told her to 'Cheer up, love'. Although the 27-year-old says it was 'not by far the worst thing [she'd] experienced', it was the final straw: 'It was the cherry on the cake of all the other unwanted sexual harassment, looks, touches, all the things you assimilate into your life that go unnoticed by others, that was breaking point,' she tells me. She founded *Cheer Up Luv*, a photo series and platform which shares stories of street harassment. It was at that point she realised some of her male friends were still in the dark about the scope of the problem – to be blunt, they didn't believe it could be happening as often as she was suggesting. 'They didn't think that it was happening on the scale that it was happening, because they'd never seen it,' she says. 'I almost started the project in spite.' They have subsequently been very supportive of Hatch's work.

Hatch's experience is not the only example. In Wales, 51-year-old father Mark Hegarty, who started the non-profit organisation *What Can I Do?* to empower men to help women by running talks and campaigns, said that he hadn't realised the true extent of the problem until starting his campaign in 2021, despite claiming not to be someone who 'walks around with [his] head in the clouds': 'It's been an uncomfortable journey, let's be honest, it's opened my eyes,' he told me. Even Deputy Prime Minister (former Justice Secretary) Dominic Raab still seemed not to have got to grips with the issue in October 2021 when asked by a journalist whether misogyny should be made a hate crime by his government. He responded by confusing the basic definition of the term, saying misogyny was wrong whether 'a man against a woman or woman against a man' (misogyny only means prejudice against women, misandry is the term for against men). What hope do we have when even the men in charge don't seem to understand the issue? And why do so many men still not see the extent of the problem when it is evidently so widespread?

While the extent of these harms is entirely obvious to those who experience them, men can be shielded simply by virtue of being men. This is often described as male privilege. The term 'privilege' can be problematic as it has the instantaneous effect of making people despondent or switch off – only hearing that they have had it easier, which does not tally with their lived experience of real hardship and difficulty. Best-selling American writer Roxane Gay said in a 2014 *Time* interview: 'I think that when people hear that phrase, they start to feel defensive. They feel like they have to apologise for some things they have no control over. You can't control the fact that you are born a white man or born into wealth.' Indeed, while men cannot control that they are a man, or even feel like they benefit from it – Seyi Falodun-Liburd, co-director at feminist organisation Level Up, warns that privilege 'does not have to be felt [by a person] to possess it' – it is an important part of understanding how people can have a particular view of the world, and certain blind spots. This is not to say that men literally never witness what is happening in front of them, but they are not informed by the same experiences as women so may perceive what is happening differently even if it is right in front of their eyes.

Just because a man knows he does not present a threat to a woman, consider why a woman has good reason to be fearful given the regularity of violence, as shown by the statistics that we know are only a fraction of the reality. A fairly mundane example of such a blind spot is running habits. On quieter residential streets if it is dusky (I avoid running in the dark), I run in the road rather than on the pavement – giving me more time to spot someone approaching. On one occasion a man ran up behind me and whispered in my ear: 'You'll get yourself killed running in the road.' Well intentioned or not, I went home shaken and frustrated that he could be so ignorant as to why a woman might take her chance against cars rather than on unlit side roads.

MP Sir Bernard Jenkin described this as a 'male blindness' – a sweeping but somewhat useful term for considering the blinkers that men can wear without even realising, the frame through which they see the world. Mr Jenkin told the House of Commons: 'The main point I want to make is about the male blindness that still persists, which can so easily distort decisions… while men and women are equal, we have very different life experiences.' When your frame is set to a certain setting, it can be hard to see beyond it. This is notable in the way men often claim they'd be flattered to be catcalled in public, believing it to be complimentary, while most women experience it entirely differently. This isn't just about the comments and stares being unwanted, but women knowing that the conditions that allow men to feel entitled to a woman's attention, even if she has expressed no interest, are the same conditions that can allow those comments to escalate into physical violence if a man feels he is being rejected. It isn't a curious oddity or universal coyness that women don't catcall men; this male behaviour is a product of inequality and is experienced by many women as such. And even if a woman were to catcall a man, it would not be the same experience, the same power dynamics are not at play in that direction with all the baggage that brings along with it.

In 2014, a woman was filmed walking the streets of Manhattan, New York, for 10 hours in silence, while wearing

jeans and a crew-neck T-shirt to record the casual street harassment she was subject to. The filmmakers documented 100
instances of verbal comments that didn't include countless winks
and whistles. On more than one occasion individual men walked
alongside her for upwards of five minutes, trying to get her attention – despite her never interacting with them. This isn't about
flattery, it's a demonstration of power. In 1972, art critic John
Berger wrote in *Ways of Seeing*: 'Men look at women. Women
watch themselves being looked at.' Another visual representation
of a flipped male view is a series by photographer Nacho López.
In 1953, Lopez hired an actress to walk through the plazas of
Mexico City and took photos of men reacting and leering at her.
The photos hold a mirror up to men's behaviour as seen by the
woman rather than by the man. When we consider that men and
women's different experiences of the world inform their outlook
it is perhaps easier to understand why for many men the extent of
what is happening around them – even to the women they share
their beds or their blood ties with – remains unseen.

When beginning on this journey it is important for men to
consider that their experience of the world is not universal and
as such the way they might feel about a certain behaviour – it's
a joke, banter or just for fun – might rightly not be shared by
women. As the statistics show, violence against women happens
on a phenomenal scale all around us. This happens every day,
in our streets, our towns, possibly in our family or our friends.
Men's violence doesn't just happen in breaking news alerts or

distant lands with different men. We must accept it happens, whether it is seen by men or not.

Similarly to doing anti-racist work, even if men do not witness the problem, it doesn't mean it isn't there. And men must see that it is a gendered crime. It isn't a coincidence that so many of the perpetrators are men and so many of the victims are women. As men begin reassessing, it is important to keep these numbers in mind; the imbalance they clearly demonstrate and the subsequent fallout for women in the way they live their lives. Margaret Atwood, author of dystopian fiction *The Handmaid's Tale*, famously said in a 1982 speech at the University of Waterloo: 'Men are afraid women will laugh at them. Women are afraid men will kill them.' Forty years later, the situation has not changed.

2

Understand It is a Spectrum

In 1976, a strange advert appeared in the personal pages of newspapers across Los Angeles. The headline asked simply: 'Are you a rapist?' It was followed by a very brief explanation: 'Researcher interviewing anonymously by phone to protect your identity. Call 213 ---.' The unconventional phone line was open from 9 a.m. to 9 p.m. and was run by Samuel D. Smithyman, a PhD candidate at Claremont Graduate University, a school in a suburban city to the east of LA county.

Smithyman, who later became a clinical psychologist, told a *New York Times* reporter in 2017 that he wasn't expecting any men to actually ring him. But they did. Nearly 200 times. Over the course of the 182 phone calls, he was able to conduct 55 complete interviews ranging in length from 30 to 50 minutes and asked 122 questions. The survey focused on basic demographic information as well as the experience of rape. Smithyman, who was researching for his 22-page PhD dissertation, titled: 'The

Undetected Rapist', wanted to understand more about those who rape. About their backgrounds and their motivations. These were men who had managed to avoid contact with the criminal justice system but had raped women.

On the hotline were a variety of men: a painter who had raped the wife of someone he knew, a school caretaker who described his 10 to 15 rapes as a way of 'getting even', and a computer programmer who had raped his 'sort of girlfriend'. What Smithyman drew from the interviews was that we cannot put rapists into metaphorical boxes. The reality is that men who rape do not always fit the narrow stereotypes and caricatures that popular culture and media tends to portray. The reality that Smithyman highlighted was how *normal* these men sounded, how varied their backgrounds, how they represented a cross-section of society rather than an outside group or small subset.

The findings showed that 74 per cent of the respondents had raped more than once, 70 per cent were under 24 when they committed their first offence, 50 per cent were married, 58 per cent were college or university graduates, 72 per cent had never been arrested and the callers represented the full socioeconomic spectrum from lower to upper middle classes. In short, the data concluded that 'a rapist is more *like* than unlike, the majority of American men'.

Collectively this is not the narrative we subscribe to. While it could be said that most, if not all, women have experienced male violence or know someone who has, how many men believe that their friends or family are violent actors? Instead we think about guilty men as monsters. While their behaviour certainly can be monstrous, the monster myth allows us to mentally consider these men as existing on the fringes – not in our midst. They can be separated from the pack, the rotten ones picked out one by one. But the monster myth is flawed. As pioneering educator and author of *The Macho Paradox*, Jackson Katz, said in his 2012 TEDx Talk, these men do not 'crawl out of the swamp, come into town and do their nasty business and then retreat into the darkness'. In reality, perpetrators are much more depressingly normal than that.

This book will not only explore how a range of gender inequalities sustain violence – including financial inequality, job insecurity, cultural biases and ingrained assumptions about women – but how even within violence itself a spectrum of harms feed the worst abuses. But society often fails to recognise this. Instead we allow the monster myth to cloud our vision and outlook. We resist drawing the logical conclusion that widespread numbers of victims, as we saw in the last chapter, means widespread, and varied, numbers of perpetrators.

In January 2022, Scottish MSP Karen Adam tweeted: 'Paedophiles and predators are people. Not bogey men under the bed. Not mac wearing flashers in the street, faceless and nameless. They are our family, friends and colleagues. They are not scary monsters.' But she faced intense scrutiny and criticism, showing how many are unwilling to accept this. *Sunday Times* columnist Terri White, herself a survivor of sexual abuse, wrote in support: 'The monster myth contributes to a culture in which family members, professionals and "upstanding" members of the community are too often dismissed as incapable of such atrocities.'

Even those who are looking at guilty men in the dock can struggle to reconcile it with their preconceived notions of who commits violence. Tom Meagher, husband of 29-year-old Gillian 'Jill' Meagher, an Irish woman living in Australia who was raped and murdered in the early hours of 22 September 2012, summed this up perfectly in an op-ed he wrote after the trial of his wife's killer, Adrian Bayley: 'I had formed an image that this man was not human, that he existed as a singular force of pure evil who somehow emerged from the ether.' Meagher said he had been guilty of 'insulating [himself] with the intellectually evasive dismissal of violent men as psychotic or sociopathic aberrations'. Bayley's ability to 'weave together nouns, verbs and pronouns to form real, intelligible sentences forced a re-focus,' said Meagher.

Consider even the most basic of rape myths – that of the stranger danger. Contrary to what we might believe, the majority of sexual attacks on women are not perpetrated by a random male lurking in the darkness to pounce, but by people known personally to the victim. Only 16 per cent of rapes are commit-ted by strangers, according to the latest crime survey. The most likely perpetrators are partners or ex-partners (44 per cent) and the second largest group are either friends, acquaintances, peers in the workplace or education, or someone the victim has been on a date with. And it isn't just rape – according to the Femicide Census, only 8 per cent of femicides were perpetrated by strangers. Sociologist Michael Flood tells me: '[Our] vision of what that violence looks like is very narrow. A vision of rape is a stranger leaping out of the bushes, and physically assaulting a woman, with a weapon or leaving her physically injured.'

This narrow understanding also applies to how we think about other types of abuse, like domestic abuse. While almost all would agree that a man punching his wife in the face qualifies as such, what about emotional, coercive or financial control? Limiting her contact with friends, telling her what she can wear or when to leave the house? Polling by the *Guardian* has shown young men are the least likely to recognise what constitutes abusive behaviour in domestic settings. When asked about financial control, limiting a person's access to friends or family or stalking, less than half of young men thought that constituted family violence even though it does under law. It is much easier to think of abuse as discrete physical acts, like hitting, not as a more accurate wide-ranging continuum of everything from installing spyware on a partner's phone to telling them what they can and cannot wear when they leave the house.

Comforting ourselves with the monster myth allows us to turn a blind eye to harm – not least making for easier family meals or looking at ourselves in the mirror – but it has the consequence of allowing this harm to go on indefinitely, causing further pain to both women and men. The Femicide Census says that almost half of the men who killed women in the UK in the 10 years between 2009 and 2018 were known to have a history of violence against women, either the woman they killed or someone else. In the US, one of the biggest predicting factors for mass shootings is a man with a history of domestic abuse: between 2014 and 2019, 60 per cent of shooting incidents with four or more casualties were a result of someone who was known to be violent in the home. Years before Wayne Couzens killed Sarah Everard, his colleagues had given him the nickname 'the rapist' because he made women feel so uncomfortable. He was also linked to a report of indecent exposure at a McDonald's just days before Everard's murder (police later admitted he might have been identified as a threat sooner). When we see violence only in the world of monsters, we refuse to acknowledge what is happening right in front of us.

As well as resigning ourselves to its continuation, ignoring the problematic behaviour we see fails to acknowledge the potential for escalation of that behaviour as the men who begin with 'gateway offences' can progress to more serious crimes. A third of upskirting offenders (those who take non-consensual pictures underneath another person's clothing, normally a skirt or dress) are behind other 'serious sexual crimes' such as child abuse or sexual assault, says the Crown Prosecution Service (CPS).

These are the canaries in the coalmine, if only we'd bother to listen.

In the UK media we frame it as contradictory, rather than customary, that rapists and killers are fathers and husbands, brothers and friends. A headline on the *Daily Mail* website describing murderer and serving Met police officer Wayne Couzens, said: 'Devoted father, husband and police officer who hid dark desire to rape and kill'. Another headline, this time on *The Sun*'s, described an unnamed man who raped and abused his own daughter for 16 years as 'Monster dad'. Although this might seem like a small point about tabloid semantics, allowing the monster myth to be a central pillar of how we understand violence against women and girls has very real consequences, primarily because it allows us to put distance between ourselves and perpetrators rather than seeing everything on a spectrum of interconnected harm. If they are monsters rather than one of us, we don't have to look at what might be prompting such behaviour. The media also regularly fails to contextualise stories of violence as part of a wider movement. They treat each case as a singular example of freak individuals. From here we easily fall into the dichotomy of good and evil – nice guys (who we all know) and bad guys (who we don't) – rather than the far more accurate spectrum of violence with degrees of harm.

In Emerald Fennell's award-winning 2020 black comedy thriller, *Promising Young Woman*, we see how fragile this binary 'nice guy' and 'bad guy' setup is. The protagonist Cassie (played by Carey Mulligan) acts out a revenge fantasy to avenge her best friend, Nina, who died by suicide after being raped at medical school. Cassie says: 'Every week I go to a club and every week I act like I'm too drunk to stand. And every week a nice guy comes over to see if I'm okay.' These men regularly take Cassie home and attempt to take advantage of her before she sits up – stone-cold sober – to confront them. In one particular scene, Neil (played by Christopher Mintz-Plasse) defends himself after being caught, saying: 'I'm a nice guy', to which Cassie replies: 'Are you?'

Dr Stephen Burrell, an assistant professor in the Department of Sociology at Durham University, who completed his PhD on men's violence, says that it still makes us uncomfortable to look at perpetrators as our neighbours and friends, so instead we think about pathological monsters. Burrell says: 'It is difficult enough to accept that we might know women who have been subjected to this, but to think that actually some of my friends, my family members, my colleagues, or men I know, could be doing this in one way or another … once you start going down that road, it's difficult.' Clare McGlynn, a professor of law at Durham University, who specialises in researching image-based abuse, says this is why widespread movements such as #MeToo can be so confronting: '[Men] still try to construct it as certain types of people, certain types of men who are not them.'

In January 2018, Babe.net published an article about a woman given the pseudonym Grace, recalling a date with *Parks and Recreation* actor Aziz Ansari that turned into 'the worst night' of her life. Grace accused Ansari of sexual misconduct at his flat, claiming he ignored her verbal and non-verbal cues that she wasn't interested in sex. Ansari later said in his comedy special, *Right Now*, that he 'felt terrible that this person felt this way'. He also issued a statement explaining his position in more detail: 'We ended up engaging in sexual activity, which by all indications was completely consensual … The next day, I got a text from her saying that although "it may have seemed okay," upon further reflection, she felt uncomfortable. It was true that everything did seem okay to me, so when I heard that it was not the case for her, I was surprised and concerned. I took her words to heart and responded privately …'

The case hit a nerve, drawing up dividing lines between those who thought Grace had a point and those who categorised it simply as a bad date (some more venomously suggesting it was opportunistically being shoehorned onto the #MeToo bandwagon). It showed us how much we rely on the monster myth to separate some men from others. When those lines feel more blurred, instead of interrogating why such an event could have happened, how men and women can come away from a situation having endured such different experiences, we close ranks. We claim that the rules have suddenly changed and men are subject to scrutiny under new terms and conditions they did not sign up to. In episode three of Apple TV's drama *The Morning Show*, we see this tension. Mitch (played by Steve Carell) sits on his patio with Dick (Martin Short) – both men have been accused of sexual harassment. After initially feeling an affinity for Dick's situation, Mitch begins to perceive himself as less problematic than his friend. 'Well, you are actually a predator. And people are going to want you to own that,' Mitch bluntly tells Dick. To which Dick retorts: 'As opposed to … what are you exactly, Mitch?'

Victims can even buy into the monster myth despite being face to face with perpetrators. In 1996, 16-year-old Thordis Elva was raped by her then-boyfriend Tom Stranger, 18, in Reykjavik, Iceland, after a Christmas ball. In a somewhat controversial TED Talk the pair gave together in 2017, titled 'Our story of rape and reconciliation', Elva said: 'This incident didn't fit my ideas about rape like I'd seen on TV. Tom wasn't an armed lunatic, he was my boyfriend, and it didn't happen in a seedy alleyway, it happened in my own bed.' And for years after, Stranger also failed to see what he had done in the language of rape: 'I didn't see my deed for what it was … I gripped tight to the simple notion that I wasn't a bad person,' he told the audience. Professor Nicole Westmarland, director of the Durham Centre for Research into Violence and Abuse, says she doesn't like the term 'perpetrator' for this reason: 'It reinforces the stereotype that there is a small group of evil men out there. Yes, there are a small number of Wayne Couzens, but there's a whole load of other men who are making life, if not abusive for women, then certainly very uncomfortable and limiting their life space and freedom.'

It is also important to consider that motivations for violence against women are not as one-dimensional as we might like to imagine. They are certainly not uniformly motivated by sex.

During my cyber flashing work for *HuffPost UK*, I spoke with men who admitted sending unsolicited sexual images to women about their motives. Some were explicit in enjoying the power dynamic it established. One man, John (not his real name), spent his early twenties sending photos and said he was acting out because he wanted female acknowledgement: 'It's similar to an ignored toddler drawing on the walls or a neglected puppy or dog chewing up items they usually ignore,' he said. Another agreed it was attention-seeking, concealed under a veil of naivety about not knowing what women want: 'A cat drags a dead mouse home to its owners as a gift. Cat thinks it is doing something good but the owners don't like it sometimes.' Others revealed their sexual frustration outweighed any empathy for women. Sean said: 'I was too impatient, and if [after a brief chat] I didn't get a response, I'd sometimes send a dick pic. My logic at the time was, well, they have already lost interest so what do I have to lose?'

If we allow the monster myth to take hold then it not only shapes our understanding of who can possibly commit the worst offences but it also stops us understanding how a whole spectrum of behaviours and motives feed into a culture of violence against women. Take rape jokes: numerous studies have observed a connection between such 'humour' and real-world action. A 1998 study found that the enjoyment of sexist humour was positively correlated with rape-related attitudes and beliefs, the self-reported likelihood of forcing sex and psychological, physical and sexual aggression in men. A 2019 study from the University of Granada in Spain also found that exposure to sexist humour creates a context in which some men feel comfortable expressing aggressive tendencies towards women (i.e. self-reported rape proclivity). In March 2022, a TikTok trend emerged that played on violence against women for 'humour'. The young men in the videos imagined date scenarios that ended up, inexplicably, with the woman dead, for example: 'Imagine we went on a fishing date and I drove you out into the middle of the ocean and put you in a trash bag and threw you overboard by accident.' Or: 'Imagine we went on a laser tag date but I used a real gun and you died.' The videos racked up thousands of views. These types of 'jokes' both normalise and minimise harm against women. It makes violence an acceptable form of comedy. Although it is hard to see how such punchlines are that funny when nearly 10 per cent of all rapes and assaults in England and Wales *are* committed by someone the person has been on a date with.

If harms are only seen as living in distinct silos rather than on an interconnected scale, it is easy to ignore how things that we all do, or allow, in our day-to-day lives contribute, even in small ways, to the overall problem. Janey Starling from feminist organisation Level Up, told me: 'Violence sits on a spectrum from humiliation in the workplace and catcalling, to sexual assault, to rape, to murder, to the way that newspapers talk about murder, to the way that our culture often will blame women for their own deaths. It all reproduces control.' If we only have two opposing poles of good guy and bad guy rather than shades of grey, that allows all men to feel less accountable for the times when perhaps they should have behaved differently. Without seeing this spectrum we fail to understand how all men can make every act of violence more or less likely to happen through their behaviour.

The monster myth allows for exceptionalism. It lets the majority of men see themselves as the good ones and therefore totally at a distance from the problem. To truly tackle this means men must step back and see the thread, the spectrum, that runs through it all, how living in this society means being exposed to misogyny and sexism, how easy it is for men to adopt the parts of that system that work in their favour (often without even realising), how society can even reward men for doing so, and how resisting this takes consciousness-raising, work and unlearning.

3

Forget #NotAllMen

Because yes it's not you that would rape, bruise or kill,
But we told you who did — and yet somehow you still
Found a way you could centre yourself in our strife
And she wasn't a daughter, a sister, a wife,
She wasn't just someone for someone to own, she belonged
to herself and had worth all alone.
'Not All Men', Len Pennie, Scottish poet, 2021

A WhatsApp message pinged onto my screen. It was late March 2021, a Sunday morning, and I was waking up slowly, given we were in another lockdown and there was little else to do but sleep, eat and walk around the block. The text was from my best friend, who had sent over a link and a single question: 'Have you seen this?' It had been over a decade since we were school (and later, university) students together, but the website she shared brought memories flooding back. It was testimony after testimony from students at our school – which is boys only until sixth form, when it becomes mixed – with claims of misogyny, sexism, harassment and sometimes assault they'd experienced from peers. Collated by former pupils, Kezia Mbonye, 21, and Imogen Greenwood, 22, *KEGS Survivors* documents things that allegedly happened in classrooms, canteens, corridors, charity balls and other places where students are supposed to be safe. I hadn't seen it and spent the next few hours reading through the 100-plus posts.

Some detailed house parties when girls were drunk and coerced into bathrooms, where boys forced a kiss before allowing them to leave, having their genitals grabbed under the table in lessons, the sexualisation of female students in their uniform, rankings based on attractiveness and open discussions of private sexual behaviour seen as fair game for public ridicule. Although my memories of school were largely good, the website prompted some notable recollections: a student speech to our entire year that made sexual jibes at my (and others) expense; an ongoing 'joke', where boys would shout 'Shut up!' at their girlfriends when they were speaking, and a group placing a bet on who could be the first to sleep with a Black woman. I was never sure if this actually happened or was just talk, but either way this intersection of racism and sexism seemed entirely believable, a prime example of what feminist scholar Moya Bailey described in 2010 as 'misogynoir', where race and gender both play roles in discrimination, compounding the impact on the few women of colour in our cohort.

As I scrolled, I noticed the testimonies were anonymous but scant details shed light on the author's ages, demonstrating that these experiences were not exclusive to one year group at a particular time, or one friendship circle. They were not blaming a batch of bad apples operating in shady dark corners. Instead, the submissions spoke of how the environment was a petri dish. They did not suggest that everyone was guilty of the worst offences but a recurring theme was the large-scale complicity. The type of complicity that comes in many forms, from laughing along and joining in to keeping silent. The behaviour was so normalised that most took it as status quo even if they might privately have had reservations or struggled to cope. Indeed, I'm sure that I myself was guilty of internalised misogyny at that time.

Most of the testimonies are from victims, but others are from the perpetrators, retrospectively begging for the adults in the room to have done more, to have said more, made those behaviours a teachable moment.* Given the more than 50,000 testimonies now up on the national *Everyone's Invited* website, which allows similar anonymous submissions from students across educational settings, it is clear my alma mater isn't alone in facing this reckoning.

In the post-#MeToo era, we see a friction between the idea that new learning has allowed old actions to be seen in a different

---

* The school has since responded to the testimonies by re-designing *PSHE*, with the two pupils running the website, and has introduced a number of other measures, saying it had been a 'very painful time' and it was determined to bring 'constructive change'.

light and that it is only public pressure acting as a catalyst for faux-remorse, not genuine reassessment. In Amia Srinivasan's *The Right To Sex*, she writes: 'Those who insist that men aren't in a position to know better are in denial of what men have seen and heard. Men have chosen not to listen because it has suited them not to do so, because the norms of masculinity dictate that their pleasure takes priority, because all around them other men have been doing the same.' Whether you agree with Srinivasan's analysis, or are willing to give a little more benefit of the doubt, especially to school-aged boys, it is clear that, as discussed in the previous chapter (*see also* p. 30), even those who see themselves as innocent of violence against women can help to – directly or indirectly – foster a climate in which this behaviour is seen as totally admissible.

At this point in the book, some men might have accepted that men's violence exists but are struggling to see themselves as personally involved. This might partly be because of the language we use, like 'violence against women' or 'women's issues', which, despite centring victim-survivors, author Jackson Katz says signals to men that they can switch off – lumping it in with news about smear tests and tampons. This linguistic set-up of the phrase 'violence against women' not only fails to address men as the most likely perpetrators, as the statistics tell us, but conjures up ideas of the violence as just happening in the ether, existing in the air around us (or by monsters who we do not know). The language tells us violence is done to someone, but not done *by* someone. Language is crucial because the way that we talk about things informs how we unconsciously think about those things: we see it as representing neutrality.

But even if we go beyond this linguistic argument and reframe violence against women more explicitly as men's violence, some men might be tempted to say, 'not all of us'. To list good guy credentials to feel exempt from such a critique. In a (rather unscientific) Twitter poll, I asked my male followers why they were not doing more to help with this issue, adding pointedly that I didn't want to know if they thought they were. This did not stop tens of men dropping into my DMs to list their efforts, some to solicit praise. It is understandable many feel by presenting evidence of good behaviour they can be excluded from frustrating generalisations, but it is crucial to see how this #NotAllMen-style argument is unhelpful as we start to do this work.

At the most basic level, #NotAllMen is used as an autopilot retort when statements are made about men's violence. Its exact origins are not clear, but by 2014 it was being used widely enough to become the subject of internet ridicule, with feminists deploying it as joke fodder. Artist Matt Lubchansky sketched the fictional 'Not All Man' superhero who, upon seeing the 'man signal' projected onto the night sky, rushes to a phone box to change into his fedora and smashes through a cafe window, where two women are talking. 'May I play devil's advocate,' he shouts as glass shatters on the floor around him. Other memes have featured characters from Jaws the shark to the Kool-Aid jug appearing at unsuspecting moments to declare: 'Not All Men!'

In May 2014, following a mass shooting in Isla Vista, California, by 22-year-old Elliot Rodger, #NotAllMen was arguably at its most visible. Rodger killed six people, and injured 14 others, some outside a sorority house, and was a member of the misogynist incel 'involuntarily celibate' community. Before the shooting, Rodger had posted a 141-page manifesto detailing his absolute loathing of women and frustration at his continued virginity. He wanted to punish women as well as those he perceived as sexually successful men. After the event there was an explosion of #NotAllMen commentators, followed by a new trending hashtag #YesAllWomen, channelling the frustration at #NotAllMen and a place where women could share grief, solidarity, and detail the extent of men's violence towards women.

Despite this pushback against #NotAllMen, even now, years later, the underlying sentiment still bubbles up. A YouGov survey in 2019 shed light on this when 27,000 people were asked which of these two views came closest to their own: 'There is room for improvement among all or nearly all men and it is right to ask men as a whole to be better' or 'The problems blamed on men as a whole are only caused by a small minority and it is wrong to blame all men for it'. A huge 58 per cent chose the second option, with 29 per cent choosing the first and the remainder undecided. The focus remains on the fault of outlying individuals rather than any collective responsibility.

If we break it down, we can see how the #NotAllMen defence works effectively at exonerating men on two levels: either because men feel they are supposedly doing enough already to help, or are in no way complicit so should not have to concern themselves with resolving it. It is easy to see how both might be appealing to men. Dr Stephen Burrell says such disassociation – separating yourself from the problem – is one of the responses he most frequently encounters in his work with men and boys on violence: 'You can recognise that yes, this is terrible, but not make the connection to your own life.' He adds that he sees lots of othering of groups, who men wrongly assume are more likely to be prone to violence – groups who are already demonised in other ways like men of colour or working-class men. 'It is easier to talk about those men who are not us,' says Burrell.*

But, whatever a man's reason for using #NotAllMen, the pragmatic consequence is just to drown out the conversation or throw it off course. Similarly to white people wanting to protest their colour blindness when confronted with discussions about racism, #NotAllMen is a knee-jerk response, a leap to defensiveness. It wants the conversation to be flipped to reassure an individual, not to continue down a path about the systemic issues facing women. It's a bad faith response – a diversionary tactic to move our focus away from the questions we must answer – that men must resist the temptation to indulge when doing this work.

At best, #NotAllMen is totally unhelpful and at worst,

---

* Philosopher Amia Srinivasan writes pointedly of such racist and classist assumptions: 'Why is it when white men rape they are violating a norm, but when brown men rape they are conforming to one?'

intentionally and deliberately problematic. It serves to derail a conversation about necessary change and make the issue all about individual men. Women already know that not every man is a rapist or murderer and it is a waste of everyone's time to feel the need to constantly hammer that home. Labour MP Jess Phillips told a panel hosted by the *Independent* in January 2022: 'We're having an argument back that no feminist ever started, I've never heard anybody say all men are rapists or perpetrators.' At its most problematic then, #NotAllMen is a straw man argument, a misrepresentation of the narrative. It attempts to distort what women are arguing about gender violence in a bid to neutralise the threat that such conversations present to male dominance. A dog whistle for men who feel attacked by the centering and platforming of women's issues.

As well as deflecting the conversation, feeling the need to resort to #NotAllMen is a tell. It is someone demonstrating that they have not yet done the work to understand how, just as we saw at my school, we are all products of a society that broadly socialises men – and women – from the day they are born to expect certain behaviour without question, or at least much resistance. How violence is interwoven into our systems and disadvantages women in any number of ways, not just outright violence. My school and what happened there was merely a microcosm of this form of social acceptance.

Today, #NotAllMen can also present in other ways such as 'What about men's problems?' or 'Why are you leaving men out when talking about harm?' The disguise might be different but the bad actor remains the same. Of course these are acceptable questions to ask more broadly, but not as an impulsive response to women detailing the prejudice and inequality they face. To do so has the same effect as the original #NotAllMen by side-tracking a conversation about women's problems and trying to make it all about men. We can see examples of this during the annual International Women's Day (IWD) on 8 March. For years, comedian Richard Herring has spent the day responding to the deluge of commentators on Twitter asking: 'When is International Men's Day?' because they see IWD trending. Herring tells them simply, it is 19 November. Talking about women does not always need to be a moment to talk about men. This can even seep into institutions: in 2020 the Police Service of Northern Ireland (PSNI) defended an initiative set up for IWD in which it asked all female officers to nominate a male colleague who had supported their career. Talking about, and celebrating, women is not anti-men, it's pro-women, in a society set up for men.

For those who feel drawn to the #NotAllMen defence, it can be easier to reframe criticism as not just being about absence of bad behaviour in men, but how much men are proactively supporting women in tackling violence. Are all men doing that? Actor and former *T4* presenter Jameela Jamil tweeted in 2021: 'It's true that not all men harm women. But do all men work to make sure their fellow men do not harm women?

Do they interrupt troubling language and behaviour in others? Do they have conversations about women's safety/consent with their sons? Are all men interested in our safety?' This is the crux of the issue – that being a good guy is not enough to exonerate you from doing the work. After all, a quote (long misattributed to Irish philosopher Edmund Burke) said: 'The only thing necessary for the triumph of evil is for good men and women to do nothing.'

Because oppression can be unconscious. Feminist Peggy McIntosh wrote in her essay 'White Privilege: Unpacking The Invisible Knapsack': 'After I realised the extent to which men work from a base of unacknowledged privilege, I understood that much of their oppressiveness was unconscious.' It is important to see how all men can perpetuate inequalities through participating in larger systems that favour men and devalue women – like the economy and unpaid labour. In her 1984 work, *Feminist Theory from Margin to Centre*, feminist author and social activist bell hooks, says: 'All men support and perpetuate sexism and sexist oppression in one form or another … while they need not blame themselves for accepting sexism, they must assume responsibility for eliminating it,' recognising how men can be 'comrades in struggle'. In order for this movement to act as radical social change, which feminism inherently is, all men must feel the burden rest on their shoulders. Men do not need to feel guilty for being men, but rather feel responsible for helping to make the change. This means scrutinising one's own behaviour both present and historic and seeing how individuals uphold systems.

For some this will be realising they have heard a friend make a sexist comment but ignored it to avoid a confrontation or gave the green light for sexist jokes to continue by laughing along awkwardly. For others it will be remembering the unspoken assumption that their wife would be the primary caregiver if they started a family, or benefitting from a company that has a gender pay gap that favours its male employees. Elsewhere, men will have to accept that they did rape their girlfriend because they felt entitled to do so or thought a woman was lying when she told a story about being raped by a friend because it didn't line up with his perceptions of that man. Actor Terry Crews, who testified at the US Senate about his experience of sexual assault at a Hollywood party in 2018, summed this up: 'What we're talking about is not a conspiracy. We're talking about a complicit system. We're talking about guys who look the other way.' Silence colludes with and condones violence.

To a less cynical degree, #NotAllMen helps everyone – men and women – rationalise random violence. Dr Fiona Vera-Gray says: 'It can be a self-protective thing. It is this false belief that if we do all the right things, and the women we love do, they're not going to be victimised. It ties into another myth, which is that the world is just, essentially right and good things happen to good people. Like saying, "it's karma".' Of course believing in the righteousness of the world requires social privilege, but in a world where half of the population are subjected to such violence from the other half, sometimes such fantasies about universal justice can be appealing.

When feeling drawn to saying #NotAllMen, Michael Flood says instead these are opportunities for men to look at getting their house in order. Instead of being tempted to defend oneself, use it as a moment for change. 'That is to look critically at our own lives, and ask ourselves some of those difficult questions about how fair and equal our treatment of women has always been,' he says. 'Because many men will say, "I'm never violent towards women", but once we recognise the range of forms of violence we go, "Ah, actually I've sometimes treated my wife or girlfriend like that."' And if you still find yourself drawing a blank on any such examples in your own life, then listening to women's experiences – without feeling the need to interject with a defence – should be an easy request as scrutiny will not leave you concerned for your own reputation. If one is not worried about the fragility of their reputation.

Of course not all men are violent towards women, but if all men decided it was their responsibility to challenge violence, the violence would end tomorrow. So while addressing this necessitates targeting the men who use violence, it doesn't stop there. As we've seen, these men are not anomalies, they are far more everyday than that. But we must go further and find many allies for this movement in the men who – often without malice – condone, or are complicit in allowing, this behaviour to continue. Tackling #NotAllMen is about everyone accepting that living in a patriarchal and unequal society means having participated in elements of this, having reinforced prejudices and behaviours that make life harder for women. In being honest about this, we can stand on the start line together, in a better place to confront the social-isation of men that accepts sexism and misogyny as the norm. Being honest about past behaviour and wrongdoings rather than expending energy trying to present a flawless personal history.

This is not about just demonising men but seeing how impossibly difficult it can be to navigate a sexist society without absorbing any of those parts. Even when we believe we are reject-ing prejudiced ideas we can still be unknowingly (or knowingly) perpetuating them. This isn't always about a personal failure – gender inequality is a self-reinforcing system that has survived for centuries by appealing to a broad spectrum of people. From those who engage in the smallest of ways, to those who are content indulging the most damaging of practices. Losing #NotAllMen as a defensive shield means men have seen that for what it is and are ready to move forward.

4

Get to Grips With History

In a speech given by author David Foster Wallace to graduates at Kenyon College, Ohio, in 2005, he shared this anecdote: 'Two younger fish are out swimming. An older fish swims past them and says: "Morning, boys, how's the water?" The two young fish swim on and then eventually one looks over and asks the other, "What the hell is water?"' We cannot always see what we are swimming in, but seeing this context is crucial to understanding the shape of our lives. It is impossible to look at the current state of men's violence against women without examining the historical backdrop we operate against – the power imbalance and unequal status of women, upheld by our laws, cultural values and social norms. We do not exist in a vacuum and we are products of our environment. VAWG isn't simply an issue between two people behind a closed door, it is rooted in how our world is set up. In the next chapters we're going to see how our history, culture and ideas about men and women feed the problem and make it harder to tackle. Prepare for a potted history, a whistle-stop tour, through the world of *man*kind.

In 1949, Simone de Beauvoir wrote in *The Second Sex* that 'humanity is man and man defines women'. Historically, women have been seen as a deviation from the absolute norm of man – men by contrast are the default gender. Even in the Bible we see that women come after men when God makes Eve from the rib of Adam – the man exists first, the woman literally made from his body (despite notably women being the child bearers). Women are therefore a variety, or type, of man, a sub-branch of the original human. This centring of men may seem inconsequential but it has repercussions – the lives of men are taken to be representative of everyone. Their experience is seen as the centre of the world. Not a unique experience. From here, it is only a small step for men to be the axes off which everyone else hangs. Why wouldn't their worldview, their needs, their ambitions, their desires, be prioritised?

We can see how unconscious this male default mode is in our use of language. We use male gendered terms, such as mankind, to refer to all humans. By comparison, consider if we were to use the term womankind to refer to everyone, how exclusively female that would feel. Or the now-ubiquitous phrase 'Hey, guys' to address a mixed sex group; if it was replaced with 'Hey, gals', it would feel pointedly female and exclusionary to men in the group. When the male default is used, it equally masks women's experiences but this is taken as standard. In Caroline Criado

Perez's book *Invisible Women*, she explains: 'Seeing men as the human default is fundamental to the structure of human society. It's an old habit and it runs deep.' She uses the fourth-century BC example of Aristotle's *On the Generation of Animals* when he wrote: 'The first departure from type is indeed that the offspring should become female instead of male'.

The word patriarchy comes from the Greek *patriarkhēs* meaning 'rule of the father'. The Cambridge Dictionary defines patriarchy in two ways: 'A society in which the oldest male is the leader of the family, or a society controlled by men in which they use their power to their own advantage'. In a patriarchy, women's secondariness to men is an immutable fact. Women's inferiority is not seen as something created and sustained but something they inherently possess, like a certain shoe size. It becomes unremarkable. Make no mistake, patriarchy does not mean that no woman can be successful – the UK, for example, has so far had two female prime ministers – but those individual successes, like the success of individual Black people in a racist society, do not negate the fact that male dominance is built in: it is the factory setting.

The supremacy of men is not a biological or an evolutionary non-negotiable part of life. By looking at the origins of patriarchy we can see how it does not reflect an irrefutable state of men dominating women – perhaps because we tell ourselves they are, on average, bigger and stronger – but that it is a choice. Scientists have written that it was only around 12,000 years ago that our society moved into being patriarchal as humans moved from being hunter-gatherers to having homesteads and acquiring resources to then defend and expand. This saw men use military muscle and strength to pass assets between themselves, live in closer-knit male groups, and saw the erosion of female agency and autonomy. As this became the prevailing mode of operation, laws and cultural ideas were devised to support male superiority, the centrality of men in its very bones.

This was all about maintaining power, forcing women to stay in their own lane and not compete with men's grasp on the wheel. Jaclyn Friedman wrote in her book *Believe Me: How Trusting Women Can Change The World*: 'The delegitimisation of women's authority isn't the unfortunate side-effect of a broken framework. It's the grease that makes the entire system go. Women's erasure is an essential part of the deal powerful men have always made with the men they would have power over: let me have control over you, and in turn I will ensure you can control women.' Women being secondary to men isn't an accident, it is intentional. It is the modus operandi of a patriarchy. Men are socialised from childhood to anticipate dominance over women and to act accordingly, often without even realising.

Legislation has long been created that allowed men to dominate and use violence against women as a means of doing so. Throughout the nineteenth century in England, the phrase 'the rule of thumb' appeared in popular cartoons and print media. Although there are some disputes about the true meaning, it has been taken to mean that a man was permitted to beat his wife as long as the instrument was not wider than the width of a thumb following a judgement in 1857. Even if we dispute this definition, common law did permit a man to chastise his wife. The law of coverture meant that a husband became legally responsible for his wife and children at the point of marriage, meaning he was entitled to control their behaviour – though by 1866, laws did exist to punish men who beat their wives too harshly. In 1895, a bylaw was created in the City of London that made it illegal to hit your wife between the hours of 10 p.m. and 7 a.m., not because of the harm to the women but because the noise of women being beaten was keeping others awake. Such norms have fed ideas about domestic abuse being in the realm of private, a family matter in which people shouldn't intervene.

Laws that protect women from violence were slow coming. It was in the twentieth century – 1956 – that rape in any form was legally defined for the first time in England and Wales. Even then it was under specific criteria such as incest, under-16s or anal sex. In 1976 the first piece of legislation was dedicated to combating domestic violence. Even refuges are a fairly modern concept. The world's first refuge for victims of domestic abuse opened in 1971 in Chiswick, west London, by the charity Refuge. The 1970s saw the birth of Women's Aid, Southall Black Sisters and Rape Crisis. It was only 30 years ago that it was determined marital rape was illegal in England and Wales – a man could not have sex with his wife against her will just because she was his wife. We waited until 2015 to see the introduction of coercive control laws, introduced to strengthen the powers of the police in combating domestic abuse and dealing with cases without physical assault, until 2019 to have upskirting made illegal under voyeurism laws and until 2022 to see cyber flashing added to the online harms legislation.

It wasn't just violence legislation that historically was slow-moving, it was also laws that recognised women's personhood – rather than lumping them as an extension of their fathers or husbands. In 1964 – just three years after the rollout of the contraceptive pill (only for married women) – the Married Women's Property Act was revised to mean that women could be legal owners of money they owned and thus inherit. Prior to this, anything earned or gained would become a woman's husband's by default. As late as the 1970s working women were refused mortgages unless they could secure the signature of a male guarantor (this was the same year that the televised Miss World Competition at the Royal Albert Hall was interrupted by feminist protestors throwing flour and smoke bombs, claiming the event was a cattle market). In 1990, independent taxation for women was introduced, meaning that married women were taxed separately from their husbands. Pubs could still refuse to serve women at the bar on the basis of their sex until 1982. So many of these changes happened within the lifetimes of today's British adults, or at least their parents. Clearly the way in which our world operates is still tainted by the trickle-down effect of this. It is worth noting that in a 2016 survey, 85 per cent of British women interviewed between the ages of 18 to 30 were still going to take their husband's surname if they married. Even in the twenty-first century, one of the ultimate signifiers of person-hood – your name – still largely defers to a patriarchal practice of adopting a man's: it is not ancient history.

Historically, many decisions would have been gendered because it was only men with access to decision-making spaces and they would make decisions based on their own outlook on life. Before then having it recorded and spoken about by other men (per Winston Churchill's famous quote: 'History will be kind to me, for I intend to write it'). Even today we still see men's achievements recorded in a way that women's are not – this then means those achievements are airbrushed out of the history books, seen as not having happened. The precedent they could have set, the minds they could have changed about a woman's place in the world, never have a chance to be. It is a self-fulfilling prophecy. In the 1990s, science historian Margaret W Rossiter coined the term 'The Matilda Effect' to describe this erasure in the field of science, referencing an 1883 essay by feminist Matilda Joslyn Gage that listed many of women's inventions that have been forgotten: the aquarium (Jeanette Power), the deep-sea telescope (Sarah Mather) or the process of making marble from limestone (Harriet Hosmer).

Even when women were written about they were often fallen women or highly sexualised. Think about Cleopatra or Helen of Troy. Even Eve quickly entices Adam to eat the forbidden apple in the Garden of Eden, committing the original sin. As Jane

Austen wrote: 'Men have had every advantage of us in telling their own story … the pen has been in their hands.'

Today, there are efforts to redress this, but it is slow work, often led by individual women. Dr Jess Wade from Imperial College London has spent years adding hundreds of Wikipedia entries for women in science to reverse this trend. Elsewhere, only 14 per cent of the 950 plus blue plaques celebrating historical figures placed around London are for women – this is even with a push by English Heritage to include more. And in 2022, Bristol Cathedral finally had to replace a plaque that commemorated the first women to be ordained as priests into the Church of England in 1994. The crucial reason the plaque needed updating? It only named the male clergy who carried out the ceremony, not the 32 female deacons who were making history.

Where only men's lives are recorded and subsequently learned about, men do not need to concern themselves with understanding women's experiences. What happens to women is a niche topic or interest. This is true of even the smartest men. Consider when NASA sent the first woman, Sally Ride, into space. They thought she would need 100 tampons for a week. The fact that this was seen as a reasonable guess and not humiliating for the rocket scientists is revealing of both how few women had been involved in space exploration and how unimportant it is that men need to understand the lives of women.

Gender inequality is so enmeshed in our historical norms, interlocking with capitalism and the supremacy of whiteness (the building blocks of the British Empire) that even today we still see the long reach of its toxic tentacles. Women's representation in public life remains far from equal. In 2021, only 35 per cent of UK MPs were women – the highest that number has ever been. This number had remained steadily low since 1918, before a jump in the 1990s, but numbers alone aren't the only metric of gender progress – the 1997 Labour intake of 101 female MPs were still unhelpfully referred to in the press with sexist names like 'Blair's Babes'. And if we look across the pond, we had the White House Oval Office under President Trump filled exclusively with men making decisions about abortion access for women. A scene worthy of Margaret Atwood's Republic of Gilead and one that perfectly captures a patriarchy at play, it is hard to imagine a scenario in which a room of women leaders could legislate men's bodies.

This isn't just a political problem, in the private sector only eight of the UK's top 100 companies are headed by women. Women do now make up nearly 40 per cent of FTSE 100 top table roles – this number has been praised compared to only 12 per cent in 2012 – but it is still not equal.

Centering of men's experiences means that even our cities are designed for men's needs, prioritising roads and ways of getting to and from work in offices over doing unpaid labour like childcare or shopping that is more likely to happen on foot; making pavements and stairwells too narrow for prams; putting blind alleyways, underpasses and insufficient street lighting in urban planning that does not consider how safe women feel. The official London tube map only has three stops named after women (Seven Sisters after the Hibbert sisters, Victoria after Queen Victoria, and Lancaster Gate after another of Queen Victoria's royal titles) and many more inspired by famous men. Of the approximately 800 statues across the UK only one in five are female and even fewer of those are actually named women rather than nameless female figures. On Bank of England banknotes there have only been three women featured – Florence Nightingale, Elizabeth Fry and Jane Austen – since the 1970s, compared to 12 men. Men are everywhere and women are nowhere.

When women aren't seen, they are also then not included in decisions. In public spaces the number of toilets is based on men's needs, leaving long queues of women at theatre intervals. It isn't just the architecture either, air conditioning is set to levels too cold for women but right for men (it is set on a 1960s formula based on the metabolism of an 70kg (11st) man, while women generally work better at 3°C warmer because they generally have slower metabolic rates and are smaller) making shared areas more comfortable for men's preferences. Even smartphones are designed to be the right size for men's hands, which are generally larger. These things don't just make life inconvenient for women, they make it downright dangerous too. In medicine, women operated on by male surgeons in Britain are 32 per cent more likely to die and 15 per cent more likely to have bad outcomes than if operated on by a woman, because of implicit sex biases in medicine and an historic smaller volume of research on women. Women are 50 per cent more likely to have a stroke misdiagnosed because public perception of 'common symptoms' are based on men. Women are also less likely to be given CPR in public – with training mannequins designed to look like men. This means odds of survival for men are 23 per cent higher in a situation where they need to be resuscitated in public.

We are already seeing how inequality is being future-proofed in the development of new sexist technologies: being coded into female-sounding AI assistants, like Siri (Apple), Alexa (Amazon) and Cortana (Microsoft). UNESCO says these are given female names and voices as they are 'engineered to be uniformly subservient', including in the programmed responses like Siri's 'I'd blush if I could' remark, which the software said in response to users calling her a bitch. In 2019 it was eventually updated to a more neutral 'I don't know how to respond to that', which is still hardly inspiring. It doesn't help that Silicon Valley is a hugely male-dominated space, meaning once again women's voices are not in the room in which decisions are being made.

In Malorie Blackman's *Noughts & Crosses*, Blackman expertly creates a race-flipped world in which the white Noughts have been ruled over by Black Cross colonisers from 'Aprica' after they conquered European countries. The Nought protagonist Callum faces a lifetime of 'flesh-coloured' plasters (Band-Aids) that do not suit his skin, routine mispronunciation of his name and discriminatory policing. Blackman's fictional world is a powerful tonic for those who argue systemic racism is a fallacy or a feature of a bygone era. Similarly to how such literary role reversal can pull back the curtain on the continued existence of race inequality, it is important to see how the idea of women as second-class citizens is so baked in the foundations of our society that it can be hard to unpick, rendering it invisible – a norm that we have come to accept. Women's pain and subjugation, particularly at the hands of men, is just part and parcel of life. This is when it becomes easy to miss because it is just, well, normal.

Globally, patriarchy is the rule, not the exception, but it is important to note that it does not give men universally the same experience or benefits, as it intersects with other identities like race or class. As bell hooks wrote in *Comrades In Struggle*: 'Men do not share a common social status … all men do not benefit equally from sexism'. Those who are white, middle class, from the Global North are going to experience benefits of patriarchy that others do not, as well as those who have leadership roles, private educations or personal wealth that defers additional power and influence. Although the privilege afforded to men through patriarchy does not flatten their identities to one homogenous experience (just as there is not one single female experience), all men do benefit to a degree under patriarchy in a way that women do not.

Even as society introduces greater laws of equality, the patriarchy remains steadfast. Feminist Cynthia Enloe wrote about this in her theory of the 'sustainability of patriarchy', where she notes the way it adapts to survive – we still see strongholds of male power like certain high-profile roles (the US presidency) that have never been held by a woman. Because of this we cannot sit back on our laurels and tell ourselves this is no longer a problem – that equality has been reached, a box ticked. Indeed, the fragility of women's rights became evident in the Covid-19 pandemic – a moment of crisis – when much progress was quickly undone. UN Women estimated that the pandemic could wipe out 25 years of increasing gender equality as women began taking on significantly more domestic chores, family care and unpaid work as the worlds of home and work collided as never before. 'Everything we worked for, that has taken 25 years, could be lost in a year,' said UN Women deputy executive director Anita Bhatia.

The Institute of Fiscal Studies found mothers were 47 per cent more likely to have quit or lost their job in the pandemic and 14 per cent more likely to have been furloughed. Those who retained their jobs were more likely to be interrupted at home than male spouses or partners. Mandatory gender pay gap reporting, introduced by the government in 2017, was paused, seen as something companies could not afford to cope with. Even on policy making women were left behind, including the fudged communications around Covid vaccination in pregnancy. Initially, pregnant women were told to hold off getting the vaccine, but later, when the advice changed to say it was safe, there was no government campaign or large-scale broadcast. This meant many pregnant women continued not to get the jab long after it was safe and by October 2021, one in six of the most critically ill patients in intensive care were unvaccinated pregnant women. This missed opportunity to get those women vaccinated has been criticised as 'scandalous'.

And we cannot overlook what a UN special report described as Britain's 'boys' club sexist culture'. 'Have I seen this level of sexist culture in other countries? It hasn't been so in-your-face,' said the author Rashida Manjoo. This doesn't mean that everyone in the UK is actively choosing to perpetuate sexism every day when they wake up, but that they are socialised to see (white, middle class) men's superiority as objective neutral. The ground zero from which everyone else deviates. We only need to think of the phrase 'identity politics' – generally taken to mean those for people of colour, LGBTQ+ people or people with disabilities – to see that white, middle-class, male reality is seen as the norm from which other identities are other.

But being a straight white man is also an identity. In Grayson Perry's book, *The Descent of Man*, he helpfully sums this up: 'We live and breathe in a Default Male world,' he says. 'We can't pick [default man] thoughts and feelings from the "proper, right-thinking" attitudes of our society. It is like in the past when people who spoke in cut-glass, BBC tones would insist they did not have an accent, only northerners and poor people had one of those.' Sandy Ruxton, honorary fellow at Durham University and co-host of the *Now And Men* podcast, says: 'It is a huge challenge in getting men to acknowledge that they do have a gender.'

This is a not insignificant stumbling block when it comes to addressing gender-based violence because it is perceived by many as only an issue for those who possess a gender (i.e. women or non-binary people), thus giving men permission to tune it out. This othering also perpetuates false (but convenient) notions of violence against women and girls being a marginal, or minor, issue. This is despite women currently outnumbering men in the UK at 51 per cent of the population.

Sophie Walker, founder of the Women's Equality Party, tells me: 'The male frame is something that we all exist in every day, no matter to what extent it chafes and bruises and hurts many of us … there is among many men a fundamental ignorance that they live in a world designed by and for them.' As we move into this second stage of the book men should start seeing themselves as gendered beings who have a particular, and distinct, lived experience that does not necessarily ring true with everyone else moving around in the world. Our history has set the stage for the male frame of reference to be seen as standardised, but it is not. This is upheld by other arenas, like the economy, which still relies on women subsuming the majority of unpaid labour (childcare, care for elderly parents).

By understanding the centrality of men as a societal choice we can see how this is not about making men the enemy, but showing how men were born into a system that automatically favours their experience, gives them powers and privileges denied to women, and that behaviour can become tainted and twisted by this, often without any cognitive recognition.

Inequality is woven through society like a golden thread. When we stand in some positions it is totally missable, indistinguishable from the rest of the cloth. It just looks like a part that should be there. But in other moments, with the benefit of a different perspective, we can see these strands actually stand out; they don't look right. But they are not easily tugged out with a single pull because they are everywhere, so much of the cloth's design was based around them.

5

Learn About The Gap

Only a fleeting moment, a passing comment in a long conversation, but I was sure I'd heard him correctly. We were sitting outside, across a table from each other, drinking tea and having a preliminary chat ahead of me conducting interviews to fill an open position at the company we both worked for. We'd gone over the skillset we were hoping to find and then he said – as casually as talking about breakfast – that we should not hire a woman who 'looks like she might get pregnant' (whatever that means). I was shocked, but it was presented so matter-of-factly, so unashamedly, that I thought perhaps I'd simply got the wrong end of the stick. I hadn't. To my shame and regret, I said nothing and just nodded back at him meekly.

Here in the UK, it is against the law not to give a woman a job because she is pregnant or might become pregnant. Under sex discrimination laws, employers cannot use this as a reason to deny a candidate a job. This does not mean it doesn't happen, as per my embarrassing example and sampling from research group *Pregnant Then Screwed*, which has collected hundreds of such examples of discrimination. Examples include women being told in interviews that given they already have one child there is concern about a second coming along in due course, or being told they are not committed to their work if they need to pick up children from school at the end of the day. How often do fathers face such questions in interviews? Is it even seen as relevant when interviewing middle-aged men?

Employers aren't even ashamed of this: in a survey conducted by the Equality and Human Rights Commission (EHRC), most UK employers (59 per cent) said they believed a woman should have to disclose if she is pregnant during the recruitment process. And 46 per cent said it was reasonable to ask if she has small children. The remaining statistics were equally bleak, with 40 per cent claiming to have been privy to at least one pregnant woman 'taking advantage' of their pregnancy in the workplace (it does not detail exactly what this might look like), and a third believing new mothers to be 'generally less interested in career progression'. Rebecca Hilsenrath, EHRC chief executive, said these findings showed that a lot of companies were 'in the dark ages'.

You might be wondering why all this is relevant when we're discussing violence against women? Well, as previously said, context is vital. As well as the historic and cultural barriers faced by women that we discussed in the last chapter, there are systemic financial and employment obstacles for women to navigate from the cradle to the grave. They are further symptoms of a society which has no problem with women's second-class position as a tool for exploitation and the persistent undervaluing of their contribution to economic life. These issues are overlapping circles on a Venn diagram of experience. Janey Starling of feminist organisation Level Up says: 'Patriarchy, white supremacy, homophobia all intersects with capitalism. There's so much oppression that we have inherited intergenerationally.' Although intersecting identities like class and race mean many men also suffer and struggle under capitalism, we must appreciate how our economy is generally set up in men's favour – even if it doesn't always feel that way. When we are content with giving women a worse lot in any sphere – particularly economically – it means the conditions are set for maintaining and supporting men's superiority.

Since 1970, and the introduction of the Equal Pay Act, it has been illegal to pay men and women differently for the same job: equal pay for equal work. This applies to both pay and conditions of employment, including basic salary, pension, working hours, annual leave, holiday, overtime, sick pay. It applies to employees, apprentices, agency workers, full-time, part-time or temporary contracts. If this happens, it is against the law. But the gender pay gap is different. The gender pay gap is calculated by the UK government as the difference between average hourly earnings of men and women across all jobs, not between people doing the same jobs. This then takes into account general trends for men to be given more of the higher-paid or senior jobs within organisations, while women do the less well-paid jobs.

The gender pay gap in the UK has been slowly declining, but it remains in place. The most recent data, which was taken during the coronavirus pandemic, was impacted by the large number of people on furlough. But it found the gender pay gap between women and men in full-time employment remained at 7.9 per cent. In 2019 (before Covid) this was at 9 per cent. Among all employees (not just those in full-time employment) the gap increased to 15.4 from 14.9 per cent in 2020, but was down from 17.4 per cent in 2019. Although we are seeing movement in the right direction, it is still the case that women generally earn less money than men. There is a date in the final quarter of every year – usually in November (it was 18 November in 2021) – that the Fawcett Society marks Equal Pay Day, the point in the year that women effectively stop earning, relative to men because of the gender pay gap. Although a symbolic date, it is effective at demonstrating the real-term impact of the gender pay gap, a chunk of time unpaid, and the cumulative power that this has over a lifetime of earnings.

In efforts to close the gap and increase transparency, since 2017 it has been a requirement for companies in the UK with over 250 employees to share internal pay gap reporting with the government. This data is then published. During the pandemic this reporting was halted – seen as something companies could not afford to deal with – but it has now started up again. In the past, some have seen the solution to the gender pay gap as telling individual women to be more confident, chastising them for not leaning in and pushing for pay rises like their male colleagues. But research has shown women do ask as frequently as men, they just don't get the raise. This is not about individual confidence but about institutional and cultural problems of persistently devaluing women's contributions and worth.

Sue Fish spent her entire career in the police force working her way up the ladder to become Nottinghamshire chief constable. She retired in 2017. Fish says that throughout her career she faced sexism and misogyny embedded into the system of work: 'When I joined [in 1986] they didn't employ married women but they also didn't allow female officers to join if they were "living in sin", so they asked me to "regularise the position" with my boyfriend, which meant getting engaged. I remember it so vividly.' When Fish was promoted to sergeant in 1989 she discovered that women were given a completely separate numbering system to their male colleagues, they were not viewed as the same as the men working in the role and therefore needed to be separated out in the cataloguing of staff.

Problems of inequality are so bedded into the way we work that the Fawcett Society has asked companies to stop asking about interviewees' pay history during the job application process, which it argues only ensures legacy inequalities spill over into each subsequent job opportunity. It is a vicious cycle. One damning report by the Institute for Fiscal Studies in 2021 found that the problem is so deep-rooted, government policies have made almost no difference to the gender pay gap for 25 years. Analysis by the *Guardian* found the gap to be widening, not shrinking, in some of Britain's biggest firms, with women's median hourly rate on average 10.2 per cent less than men's, compared with 9.3 per cent in 2018. And we simply cannot make the argument that men are just more well-qualified for higher earning roles: women are now studying at university in greater numbers than men, but the Department of Education reports that female graduates still have lower lifetime earnings. Over their working lives, male graduates on average gain by £130,000 and female graduates by £100,000.

Although a small minority maintain the gender pay gap is feminist fiction, there are a plethora of reasons why women still earn significantly less than men over their careers. These include differences in the volume of caring responsibilities, where women are more likely to be required to take on childcare or the care of elderly parents (because of bias) and the infamous glass ceiling. This term was coined to describe the invisible barriers to women climbing to the top of their industry – this encompasses lots of different factors like childcare-related career breaks and sexism, but also nods to the less easily quantifiable factors such as a general culture of seeing men as predisposed to success, while successful women are fighting against the odds.

Of course, one of the periods where women are most vulnerable to workplace discrimination is when they become a parent. The 'Motherhood Penalty' is well known, with one study of

French mothers suggesting that women earn 3 per cent per hour less for every child they have, compared to those who don't have children. They did not find that men had any lost income linked to parenthood. Another study from 2009 found that women with children experienced a 22 per cent loss of earnings compared to male colleagues. And this isn't just after women give birth – a 2021 study from University College London (UCL) found those who have children earn up to 45 per cent less than those who do not for up to six years after the birth of their first child. In the first year, wages can drop by 28 per cent or £306 a month. The only exception to this – those able to avoid a drop in income – was in 'highly educated' households, where it is likely parents are outsourcing childcare to a woman on a lower income to permit a return to work.

For women who are able to return to work, this isn't without its problems. Three in four mothers (77 per cent) said they had a negative or possibly discriminatory experience with their employers during the course of their pregnancy, maternity leave and/or return from maternity leave, in research conducted by the UK government's Department for Business, Energy & Industrial Strategy (BEIS). Scaled up, this could mean as many as 390,000 mothers every single year. Around one in nine mothers (11 per cent) said they felt forced to leave their job because things were so bad. In cases where women stayed in their jobs and requested flexible work, only half were granted it. A survey of 13,000 mothers carried out by the Trades Union Congress (TUC) found one in two had had a request for flexible working turned down or only partly accepted by their current employer.

In April 2015, a policy of shared parental leave was introduced in the UK, allowing eligible parents to split up to 50 weeks of leave and 37 weeks of pay between them rather than just having one person at home and one in work. But research in 2018, three years after the change, showed of the 900,000 parents who could have taken it, only 1 per cent did. The research argued that the reasons for such low uptake could be split into a number of camps. One was a basic lack of knowledge of the scheme on the part of HR managers, which will hopefully increase over time. Another was (unsurprisingly) financial. Many of the fathers in the sample were the main earners – a factor exacerbated by the gender pay gap, but one that only helps to reinforce the gap as men stay in work and get promoted while women take time out. Of course, families could opt to rely on statutory pay but the findings showed many would take a financial hit. This is just not practical for most, especially when paying for a new baby.

Another reason mentioned by all parents in the survey was cultural barriers – continued societal expectations around the roles of each parent and 'perceived normative maternal and paternal identities'. This identity was not only felt by the new parents themselves but they said was reinforced by employers who made assumptions about the mother being the primary caregiver, as well as by the policy itself, which enshrines this assumption in the very way it works by the mechanism of 'maternal transfer' (i.e. the mother must 'gift' the father her leave), which encourages 'maternal gatekeeping', say the researchers. Even with such a shared parental leave policy in place, if the reality of the situation still leaves many women feeling there is no choice (for a number of reasons), the end result remains the same.

Once we've dealt with the problems of paid work and motherhood, we must also address the long shadow of women's unpaid and unacknowledged work – both in the home and elsewhere. In her memoir *We Need to Talk About Money*, Otegha Uwagba writes: 'Working for free is, unfortunately, an inescapable part of the female condition. Entire economic systems are predicated on women assuming the burden of responsibility for the constant trickle of low-level organisation and emotional caretaking … we are the invisible worker bees holding together family units and friendship groups, global conglomerates and entire societies.'

Women still do the majority of housework when living with a male partner, at 16 hours per week, according to a UCL study of 8,500. Men do closer to six hours. When both individuals were in full-time employment, women were five times more likely to spend at least 20 hours a week doing chores. Women also still do the majority of unpaid caring roles, such as caring for elderly parents. Of the 6.5 million unpaid carers in the UK, 58 per cent (3.34 million) are women. When you look at the percentage of 'around the clock' carers providing more than 50 hours a week, the ratio of female carers is greater, at 60 per cent. Carers UK estimates the economic value of this work is around £77 billion every year.

In 1975, Silvia Federici wrote in *Wages Against Housework* that housework is often justified as being a 'natural attribute of our female physique and personality, an internal need, an aspiration, supposedly coming from the depth of our female character' – something women just want to do. A convenient message for a patriarchy that needs women to do such work. Dr Fiona Vera-Gray told me that our economy 'depends on' women doing this unpaid labour. 'Having that traditional heterosexual unit is the very foundation of our economy,' she explains. 'The system of capitalism does rely and is based on women's inequality. It needs women's inequality in order to function. You need women to be doing this unpaid work otherwise it is not going to happen.' This includes childcare.

One of the demands of the Women's Liberation Movement in the 1970s was 24-hour free childcare (the other six demands were equal pay, equal educational and job opportunities, free contraception and abortion on demand, legal and financial independence for all women, the right to a self-defined sexuality, and freedom for all women from the threat or use of violence). Imagine how much of a difference universal free childcare, 24 hours a day, would make to the inequalities women face. Particularly in the UK, where childcare costs are the third most expensive in the world (after Slovakia and Switzerland), according to data from the Organisation for Economic Co-operation and Development (OECD). To remove the choice of working but paying nursery bills that in many cases can be as much as half of a working parent's pay packet, on an average salary, or staying at home missing potentially years of your career. Even more so if you have more than one child.

Another burden on women is the much-discussed hidden mental load. Depicted in the cartoon 'You Should Have Asked' by the French artist Emma, this is the unseen managerial role often assigned to women in the home. It suggests that even as we might think household admin is more broadly shared between men and women in modern homes, the remembering to do so is an unseen weight only taken on by the woman. Assigning men tasks signals a more equal division of labour on the surface but is actually concealing this project management. As well as the mental load, feminists have argued that men's inability to share their emotional baggage with other men means that women in intimate relationships are also burdened with helping them unpack this – in 2016, Erin Rodgers referred to it as 'emotional gold digging'.

In our economic system, thousands of women are performing numerous jobs simultaneously, some paid but many others uncompensated. The sort of work that is never complete, never rewarded, mostly never even noticed. It has been sold aspirationally as 'having it all', but as per the famous saying about dancer Ginger Rogers doing everything Fred Astaire did but backwards and in high heels, women can find themselves needing to do everything men do (but better) while carrying endless hidden burdens that only compound the difficulty.

Even in economic policy at a state-wide level, women are cheated. Women are disproportionately hit by austerity policies, including changes to Universal Credit (UC) and cuts to public-sector services and jobs because more women than men work in the public sector. Women are also more likely to have low-paid jobs that mean they (and their dependents) rely on UC. If payments are reduced or removed, they are more likely to be first hit, especially single mothers. During the Covid-pandemic it was clear that women had not been taken into consideration during contingency planning (often presumably because there are fewer women at the decision-making table), with the Coronavirus Job Retention Scheme (CJRS) and the Self-Employment Income Support Scheme (SEISS) both 'overlook[ing] the specific and well-understood labour market and caring inequalities faced by women', according to the government's own analysis. Even the gendered tampon tax – that categorised tampons as luxury goods worthy of VAT – took until June 2021 to finally be removed. In the last decade of cuts, over 50 per cent of refuges for ethnic minority women have either been forced to close or taken over by an alternate provider due to lack of money.

In 2021, the World Economic Forum estimated that the deadline for closing the global gender gap had been pushed back yet another generation by the Covid-19 pandemic, from 99.5 to 135.6 years. No woman or girl alive today will see that. As with other systemic problems, individuals are not going to be able to change this single-handedly, but men should make efforts to see how this is interlaced with the issue of violence and inequality.

Having an awareness of this gap, and placing our economic system under the analytical microscope, shows us how society tolerates women's subservience more broadly. Men should be open to having conversations about this – about how women are perceived as a collective, the roles they are assigned and the conditions our capitalist society is content for them to live under – because it is here we can start to see how violence against women is also tolerated.

On an individual level men should be thinking about division of labour in their own home and whether automatic assumptions have ever been made about women as the primary caregivers. Are men really also doing the unseen labour, including unpaid care and household work? The cleaning, the tidying, the washing, the household budgeting or food shop, the frankly endless administrative organisation that is modern living. And not just executing this, but carrying the mental load of knowing it needs to be done, the remembering to do it without being prompted or corralled. This applies whether children are already on the scene or are just a future prospect. Men should also be open to greater salary transparency with their female colleagues in the workplace, to push their company to address existing gender pay gaps (and make the data public if it is not) and consider campaigning for more accessible and affordable childcare or other care-giving support that would benefit all women.

Without stepping back to look at women's position with a 360-degree view that takes in labour and capitalism, it will always be hard to fully understand the systemic nature of men's violence, how it happens with such regularity against women, why it can often feel tolerated even when it appears to be right out in the open and how to actually make it stop. But beyond participating in systems, we must also consider how men are taught to be as individuals. Could that be part of the problem, too? We have seen the rights and rewards bestowed upon them under patriarchy, but what are the expectations in return for upholding that end of the deal? Yes, men can be rewarded by a realm of power and influence, but does that kingdom come with unscalable fences that trap men as well as excluding women?

6

Examine Your Masculinity

Ryan Hart, 30, and Luke Hart, 32, grew up in a house dominated by their father. Along with their younger sister, Charlotte, and their mother, Claire, the family lived on eggshells. 'We always had to be thinking about what we were doing and how he would respond,' Ryan tells me over Zoom from his home in Surrey, where he now lives with his brother and their two dogs, Indi and Bella. 'Even things like his breathing. We monitored that because a deep breath was a sign he wasn't pleased with what we were doing.' His father's behaviour would now be classed as 'coercive control' – it included psychological torment and controlling Claire's spending, even on something as small as a coffee and bus fare while he spent £500 on a bicycle that sat unused. Although Ryan says he knew a better life was possible, he didn't understand the situation as abuse.

'I think [it was] because he was never physically violent, but he was ticking every single box [for] coercive control. At school we had a presentation from the NSPCC but they only covered being physically or sexually assaulted and so I thought this doesn't apply to us,' Ryan says. 'We didn't fully understand the red flags we had been experiencing. You never think you're living with a murderer-in-waiting.' On 19 July 2016, a few days after the boys had helped Claire and Charlotte finally move out of the family home in Spalding, Lincolnshire – statistically, leaving is the most dangerous time for an abused woman — Lance Hart shot his wife and daughter in the Castle Sports Complex swimming pool car park before turning the gun on himself.

The killings made national news and the usual tropes quickly became apparent. Columnists tripped over themselves to use phrases like 'understandable' in describing a so-called crime of passion activated by the women leaving. The familiar monster myth enveloped analysis, unable to make sense of one neighbour describing Lance as a 'very nice guy' and 'always caring'. Ryan says: 'We have such low expectations [of men], he's still a good guy, because he once volunteered or helped a neighbour fix a lightbulb.' As previously discussed, in these moments of tragedy we frame such men as both an aberration, unlike any other man, and at the same time an everyday man only one bad rejection or trigger away from homicide.

But this was not red mist descending or a fuse blown as we often like to claim in the aftermath of such tragedies, says Ryan. Shortly before he killed his wife and daughter, Lance bothered to buy a pay and display ticket to park his car in a bay. 'He was very comfortable in following rules, he knew he was going to kill but still wanted to purchase a ticket to be a good citizen, it showed the level of control he did have over himself,' Ryan explains. In fact, Lance felt fully able to justify his actions – he penned a long letter in advance, detailing the reasons for the killing, including that his wife and daughter had taken the tomato ketchup from the fridge when they moved out. He felt personally attacked by this and saw that what he did subsequently as a proportionate response, justified by his core beliefs and perception of himself as a man.

Although we should not attempt to explain away violence with one-dimensional factors, when looking at how to improve the problem of violence against women, we have to start right at the beginning, at the very notion of what men are taught it means to be a man in the modern world. We have seen how systems are set up to favour men as the default, but how are they told to be? What are men told they deserve and have a right to claim? How are masculinities defined and rewarded? What are men instructed is part of the social contract they sign in order to be a 'proper man'? How should they act? Although the Hart family example is extreme, it does show how men's ideas about themselves can transform into real world action: reality, not fiction.

Masculinity and femininity are generally understood to be socially constructed: a constellation of ways that we are taught we should shape ourselves to present to the world. There is not one universal masculinity, masculinities are relative to cultures, communities and socio-economic groups or even more narrow classifications such as within a certain sporting culture. Despite this, there are general traits we see men and women being conditioned to adopt – binary ways of behaving in supposedly gendered ways. Some are positive traits, but studies suggest there is a distinct correlation between some masculinities and violence. Sociologist Michael Flood tells me: 'If you take 1,000 men, and you want to know which of those 1,000 men are most likely to ever sexually assault or to domestically abuse a partner, one thing you would want to know is their attitudes about being a man, attitudes towards masculinity … some versions of masculinity are part of the problem.' The UN Committee on the Elimination of Discrimnation Against Women regards violence against women as 'rooted in gender-related factors, such as the ideology of men's entitlement and privilege over women, social norms regarding masculinity, and the need to assert male control or power'. A 2019 government report concurred: 'There are norms and expectations we have of men and boys which enable, entitle and require them to use violence within specific settings, often as a way to (re)assert masculine power. These norms promote the idea that violence is sometimes an acceptable, necessary, even desirable response to the problems experienced by men and boys, and as a way to get respect.' And in a report by the World Health Organization (WHO), it said: 'Traditional beliefs that men have a right to control women make women and girls vulnerable to physical, emotional and sexual violence by men. They also hinder the ability of those affected to remove themselves from abusive situations.'

Seyi Falodun-Liburd, co-director at feminist organisation Level Up, says the current view we collectively hold of masculinity 'not only makes excuses for violence against women but gives it legitimacy as a part of the human condition, as opposed to a constructed social crisis that can be ended'. In short, men are made violent through socialisations into masculinity, they are not born this way. We are building men that feel entitled to use violence against women. Lance Hart definitely had fixed ideas of masculinity and his role as a father. 'He had this sense of entitlement, as a man, as a husband, as a father, his wife should never talk back, always do the cooking, the cleaning. His children owe him everything because we wouldn't exist without him and we should serve and devote ourselves to him,' says Ryan. '[Growing up], his household was extremely patriarchal. His mum didn't work, didn't drive and his father was the breadwinner.'

The phrase 'toxic masculinity' has emerged to describe forms of masculinity that are harmful to society and to men themselves, but many men hear the phrase toxic masculinity and too easily translate that to all men are toxic. While this is not what the phrase means, we must acknowledge that messaging that instantly falls on deaf ears is not that useful and should emphasise the separation between criticising some masculinities and men as a whole. In the years since the murder of his mother and his sister, Ryan has been coming to terms with his own definition.

'We [Ryan and his brother Luke] initially attributed everything our father was doing, every attribute he had, was bad. But I don't believe there is any attribute of masculinity that is inherently bad, it is about how you use them,' he says. 'We're different from our father because we fundamentally see ourselves in a different way than he saw himself.'

Like Ryan, it is important to think about where masculinity is serving you and where it is restrictive. This does not have to be extreme examples of masculinity causing violence, but men should ask whether it impacts the way they perceive themselves, the way they act in public or in a relationship with a woman, the feelings they feel allowed to express or have to suppress, the jobs or hobbies they feel permitted to pursue and the vulnerabilities or fears they can have.

One of the first questions we ask of a pregnancy is: Boy or girl? From birth we are socialising men to standards. Some research has even shown that parents talk differently to a foetus in the womb if they know it is a boy or a girl, with heavy kicks described as 'active' or 'future football player' for a boy and 'emotional' for a girl. According to the nursery rhyme, boys are made of snips and snails and puppy dog tails while girls are made of sugar and spice and everything nice. Boys, we are told, will be boys and are encouraged to physically stand up for themselves – without crying – as soon as they can talk (women can also use these excuses, socialised as they are to the same masculinities as the men around them). In *The Simpsons*, Homer tells Marge of his need to conform: 'I can't wear a pink shirt to work. Everyone wears white shirts. I'm not popular enough to be different.' Although not all men are card-carrying members of the same masculinity, because of race, class and cultures, every man is socialised that being a 'real man' looks a certain way and attempting to break away comes at a social cost.

In his 2010 Ted Talk, 'A Call to Men', Tony Porter talks about this collective socialisation using a metaphor that he calls the 'Man Box'. In this fictional box are some of the very real ways that men are taught to present since birth: don't cry or openly express emotions with the exception of anger, which is encouraged, do not show weakness or fear, demonstrate control at all times, be heterosexual, be tough, athletic, brave, do not be like a woman or a gay man, make decisions and never need help in doing so. This box is given to men at the start of their lives (along with jobs like being a breadwinner, being the leader of the house and being a protector of others, mostly women and children). If men step outside of the wall of the box they risk alienation from peers and being viewed as weak or 'not manly enough'. Instead they must persistently strive to live up to its high standards in their everyday lives and relationships. At the very core of masculinity is that it is hard to win, but very easy to lose – and men must fight to retain it or risk losing their very sense of identity.

Mike Taggart MBE, 40, is the strategic domestic abuse officer for North Wales and ambassador for White Ribbon, a group that aims to end male violence against women. In 1997, he saw his mum, Donna Crist, killed by her husband in a domestic abuse case. Taggart was just 15. He now works with men and boys and uses a similar cardboard box metaphor to Porter. In his holdall of masculinities are things like eats meat (notably not a 'soy boy' – a pejorative term used mainly in right-wing online spaces to describe men lacking these characteristics), watches football and drinks beer. In his documentary film *The Man Card*, Jackson Katz charts how American presidential candidates have often played on manhood and masculinities to secure voters, particularly white, working-class men. A lot of candidates campaign as a 'tough guy' on crime, unafraid of military action, a protector father figure. This strategy works by capitalising on fear that some versions of masculinity are being eroded (and directs that anxiety towards women and people of colour) while ignoring where their real vulnerability lies: in a modernising economy.

In *The Descent of Man*, Grayson Perry describes the 'Department of Masculinity' that self-regulates every man: 'Somewhere in every man's head there is a governor, an unconscious inner voice sending instructions through the intercom. This governor is the boss of every man's personal branch of the Department of Masculinity. This department wants to maintain standards.' Perry believes that for too long masculinity has been a straitjacket that only serves some men, but leaves many lacking: 'What about all the teenagers who think the only manly way out of poverty and dysfunction is to become a criminal? What about all the lonely men who can't get a partner, have trouble making friends and end up killing themselves? What about all the angry men who inflict their masculine baggage on the rest of us?' He says that changing our idea of masculinity would help those suffering under it. In her ground-breaking #HeForShe speech given to the United Nations in 2014, actor Emma Watson said: 'We don't often talk about men being imprisoned by gender stereotypes but I can see that they are.'

We've touched on how the proliferation of these masculine norms becomes a problem for women in the form of violence. While this should be incentive enough to move away, seeing how some parts of masculinity fail men too should compel even the most reluctant. We don't often ask men what they struggle with as men. When writing her book, *For the Love of Men*, author Liz Plank conducted a social experiment in a park in New York city. She asked men: 'What is hard about being a man?' The response was perhaps surprising. She told *GQ*: 'They [the men] just froze. And you could tell that not only did they not necessarily feel that it was safe to share that, they'd also never thought about it.' You might be acutely aware of how masculinities are not working for you. If not, now is the time to begin interrogating that.

Perhaps nowhere is it more obvious than in mental health and suicide rates among men. Suicide in England and Wales is three times more common among men than women, a consistent trend as far back as the mid-1990s. It remains the biggest killer of men under 45 in the UK. Around one in eight men has a common mental health problem such as depression or anxiety and men report lower levels of life satisfaction than women. Despite this, men are less likely to access psychological therapies than women: only 36 per cent of referrals to NHS talking therapy are for men (and the rest for women). Men are also less likely to disclose a mental health issue to their family and friends, with only a quarter having told them during a month of it arising compared to a third of women. More than a third of men waited more than two years or never told anyone about the problem. A lot of men suffer in silence.

As well as problems in speaking about mental health, men who have internalised ideas about masculinity are less likely to have other health-seeking behaviours like going to the doctor for physical problems or worries. During the Covid-19 pandemic, studies have found men less likely to wear mandated face masks – one study from Middlesex University and the Mathematical Science Research Institute at Berkeley found men considered wearing a mask 'shameful, not cool and a sign of weakness' – and there were signs of a gender gap opening in vaccine uptake, with women 10 per cent more likely to get the injection than men. One paper from Sonoma State University in California, looking at the US, summed it up: 'Men are more likely than women to adopt beliefs and behaviours that increase their risks and are less likely to engage in behaviours that are linked with health and longevity.' Again, just as with the use of violence, these traits aren't a biological inevitability of manhood but the result of socialisation into the parameters of masculinity.

The list goes on: men who follow traditional masculinity are less inclined to take care of the planet, men are nearly twice as likely as women to take any illegal drugs, and white, heterosexual men have been shown to have the fewest friends as they age. When they do, close relationships are often defined by unhelpful language such as 'bromance', suggesting emotional intimacy in male friendships is odd, and serves to undermine elements of the Man Box, such as 'do not appear gay or like women'. Academics have even suggested that one of the reasons so few men take paternity leave (when able to do so) – and subsequently spend less time with their kids – is because of ingrained stereotypes around masculinity and fatherhood with pressure to be the one bringing home the pay packet. All of these pressures can be exacerbated for men who are queer, non-binary, trans or have other identities seen as incompatible with the Man Box.

Research from the University of Wellington (2020) looking at the online incel 'involuntary celibate' manosphere found that – similar to Ryan Hart's description of his dad (p.90) – men are drawn to this community as a response to feelings of powerlessness in a modern setting: 'Incels negotiate their anxieties of a rapidly changing globalised world with a sense of victimisation and "aggrieved entitlement" through a worldview that understands society as set up to economically, socially, and sexually favour women.' The Man Box is not serving these men either – giving them few options to acceptably express themselves as men and leaving them disillusioned and disconnected from society as a result – not to mention creating a breed of domestic terrorist for the rest of us to deal with.

But it's not just the extreme end of the scale, many men are not being served even in the smallest of ways. What about the men who would have liked to spend more time with their children when they were growing up but felt their role was to go out and make money? Those who wanted to feel more empowered – and given the tools – to talk about how they were feeling with their friends (without feeling like they were making it awkward)? To have better understood how to channel anger or sadness without just brandishing fists or staying silent?

None of this is to say that men's suffering under patriarchy is equal to women's. Acclaimed feminist author and activist bell hooks summed this up as: 'Men are not exploited or oppressed by sexism, but there are ways in which they suffer as a result of it. This suffering should not be ignored. While it in no way diminishes the seriousness of male abuse and oppression of women, or negates male responsibility for exploitative actions, the pain men experience can serve as a catalyst.' She states clearly: 'Men do oppress women. People are hurt by rigid sex role patterns. These two realities co-exist.'

Dr Loretta Trickett, associate professor at Nottingham Law School, has a PhD in masculinities. She says that many of the masculine ideas we have within society are 'unachievable' for men. 'All boys have to navigate this journey to manhood,' she says. 'But I think there are a whole bunch of men that find it really tiresome and limiting on their own masculine identities. The real tragedy is that it prevents men from being truly who they are. It forces you to negate half your humanity.' Instead of men feeling able to fully embrace every aspect of their personality, there is pressure to only utilise and display those aspects that fit with the Man Box, like showing strength and toughness rather than being emotional or sensitive. The dominant model of masculinity is still very strong and it can be scary for men to have conversations critiquing this.

Joni van de Sand, global co-director of the MenEngage Alliance, told me that thinking about how masculinity is not serving men can inform us about entry points for this anti-violence work. This might be their sexuality, struggling with discrimination or bullying, witnessing violence in the home or in public, becoming a father, worries about other men in their life – particularly younger men and boys, or concerns about their health. It could be a mental health crisis or addiction issues that forces them to ask for help or perhaps a period of poor physical health that could have been diagnosed sooner or avoided alto-gether if men didn't feel the need to cope alone and not seek medical attention. Dan Guinness, managing director of Beyond Equality, a programme that runs workshops to rethink mascu-linities and engage men and boys, says of those who attend the sessions that many have chosen to do so because they've become parents or entered a relationship with someone that has forced them to re-evaluate: 'They've been challenged by somebody' and this challenge, while difficult, is the start of many a positive change.

Examining masculinity can be beneficial for men – allowing them to discard the parts that do not serve them, such as being tough and not asking for help, and see where they are being held to standards that are damaging and might be stopping them from being vulnerable or asking for support from those around them. Indeed, feminist author Cynthia Enloe said: 'Patriarchy isn't good for anybody. It fools those who are privileged into imagining that they have a good life.' Instead of seeing masculinity and femininity as a binary set of ideals, we should reframe our understanding as on a gender spectrum with positive aspects of both to take away. Dr Stephen Burrell adds: 'There are lots of messages that feminism is dangerous to men or an enemy of men, but I think it a gift.'

The first rule of fight club, as per Brad Pitt's 1999 film *Fight Club*, can be applied to masculinity: you don't talk about it. Unlike feminism, which has somewhat successfully expanded the horizons of what is expected of girls, moving away from just schooling in subservience, masculinity is still seen as more fixed. In a column for the *Guardian*, journalist Gaby Hinsliff said this is 'to the detriment both of those who don't fit the macho stereotype and those who will grow up to be victims of insecure male rage. "Let boys be boys" is an excellent principle. But only if we recognise the full range of things boys are capable of being when we let them.'

When we're looking at how to improve the problem of violence against women by prevention rather than dealing with the consequences, shared ideas about masculinity is a good place to begin. We must reject any notion that men are naturally more violent. This is part of the way men can be conditioned into masculinities – along with damaging tropes like being unemotional, tough and never needing help – but it could be so different. If we hold on tight to current masculinities as the way men always have to be, rather than one of many ways they can choose to be, we cede the belief that things can change for everyone. Because those alternative options could simultaneously improve the lives of men who struggle under masculinity, as well as the women who experience its brutal consequences. If we choose to take this path of change we must first acknowledge that so much of what is around us is reinforcing these messages.

7

Ask If You're Being Sold To

In 2002, BBC Radio 1 DJ Chris Moyles was hosting the station's drivetime afternoon show. This was the slot that parents and kids would catch on the journey home from school, which Moyles presented with his group of on-air friends until December 2003 when he was promoted to the breakfast show. In February 2002, during one such appearance, Moyles – styled as 'The Saviour of Radio 1' because of his high ratings – began talking about the recent 16th birthday of classical singer Charlotte Church. During the segment he told his listeners that he wanted to 'lead her [Church] through the forest of sexuality now that she had reached 16'. He was 28 years old at the time the comment was made.

The BBC defended the comments, saying they were Moyles's style of humour and were not meant to be taken seriously, but the Broadcasting Standards Commission (BSC) agreed with a listener who filed a complaint, saying the remarks were inappropriate; that the sexualisation of the Welsh schoolgirl, only just of a legal age, on primetime radio was not okay. But Moyles wasn't alone in doing this to Church: a website that posted a count-down clock to her turning 16 was taken down by her lawyers (the website has been incorrectly attributed to *The Sun* newspaper, including by Church herself during her 2011 witness statement at the Leveson Inquiry) and Church was awarded 'Rear of the Year' the year she turned 16 – a competition where winners were made to pose for photographers in tight jeans. It was also not the first, or last, time Moyles was found to have 'exceeded accept-able boundaries' on his show, particularly in regards to comments about women. He went on to refer to women as 'dirty whores' on a show in 2006, a comment deemed to have breached Ofcom rules, but did not result in a fine or penalty.

It is impossible to begin to understand how male dominance is perpetuated – and how to begin to dismantle harmful forms of masculinity in a bid to reduce violence – without looking at the social cues we are subject to every day. We have seen how historically men have been positioned as the default gender and patriarchy is present in everything from the way we build our cities to the laws we create. But what about popular culture? How are we sold ideas about what it means to be a successful man or woman? What is good manhood or womanhood? How should we model ourselves and what is acceptable? As we try to reassess what we understand about gender and how men and women should interact with each other, we must acknowledge how hard it is to separate our views from those we are fed through our televisions, radios, smartphones, newspapers and magazines, 24 hours a day, 365 days a year.

Patriarchy is powerful because it intersects with capitalism. Our culture both holds up a mirror to who we are as a society – our hopes, fears, concerns, prejudice, bigotry – and simultaneously sells us aspirational ideas about who we could be in order to get us to part with our cash. Under patriarchy, male superiority is idolised and women are objectified or sexualised in a bid to sell to them, or as avenues of entertainment. Brands rely on leveraging gender stereotypes to make money through advertising and marketing, encouraging us to spend in order to live up to trademark masculinity and femininity. Some people might think they're not impacted by culture or advertising, but Jean Kilbourne, who is known for her work on women in advertising, said in her TED Talk 'The Dangerous Ways Ads See Women', that: 'The influence of advertising is quick, cumulative and for the most part, subconscious'. Sandy Ruxton, from Durham University, co-host of the *Now And Men* podcast, agrees: 'Quite a lot of research shows that the brain is pretty plastic and we are very influenced by the environments we grow up in. Gender norms kick in at a very young age, even from early childhood despite parents' best efforts. [We] are conveying messages about what it is to be male or female.'

Messaging becomes ingrained in us by consuming this cultural material and taints what we expect to see in the wider world around us. The End Violence Against Women Coalition

(EVAW) goes further, writing that it sees 'the abuse of women in our culture is directly related to the harm many women suffer'. So, it matters that our cultural landscape remains full of examples of masculine dominance, entitlement and the degradation or sexualisation of women.

Consider Page Three, a staple of British media culture for nearly 50 years – so mainstream that Conservative MPs felt safe enough referring to the photographs of topless women (some as young as 16 or 17 until 2003 when the Sexual Offences Act made topless modelling under 18 illegal) as a 'national institution'. Page Three began in 1969 by showcasing clothed glamour models in a bid to increase circulation of Rupert Murdoch's *The Sun*, copying a format in the *Daily Mirror*. In 1970, the paper printed a fully nude woman to mark the first birthday of the feature. By the mid-1970s topless models were a regular occurrence and the format reached its peak in the 1980s, launching the careers of Samantha Fox among others.

There were numerous campaigns against Page Three: in 1986, MP Clare Short introduced a Private Member's Bill, but *The Sun* responded with a 'Stop Crazy Clare' campaign, distributing car stickers and printing unflattering photos of her, according to journalist Nick Davies in his book, *Hack Attack*. When Rebekah Brooks became editor in 2003, it was expected that she might terminate the feature, but it remained in place (it helped presumably that it was aiding the sale of the newspaper). In 2012, the No More Page 3 campaign began, but it wasn't until January

2015 that the page was finally pulled. And not before *The Sun* could put one last middle finger up to campaigners, seeming to stop for a few days before issuing a 'Clarification and Correction' with a winking topless photo captioned (toe-curlingly) as a 'mammary lapse'. Although Page Three is no more, we haven't seen the end of women's bodies being used as a way to sell papers: male interest magazines like *Sports Illustrated* still see the huge commercial value in an annual swimsuit issue asking beautiful women, sometimes athletes, to pose on the beach in a bikini.

As well as in the press, in cinema and television we are still wedded to gendered stereotypes about who is included in shows and the stories we are willing to provide a budget to tell. In her 1975 essay, 'Visual Pleasure and Narrative Cinema', Laura Mulvey created the term 'male gaze' to describe how films reflected the viewpoint of male directors. Although we've seen some progress since then, a 2018 BBC study looked at how many of the Oscar-nominated films would pass the Bechdel Test. A film passes the Bechdel Test if there are at least two named female characters who, at any one point, have a conversation with each other about something other than a man. The analysis found that fewer than half of the 89 films named Best Picture at the Oscars made the grade.

We also see films and TV shows normalising rape culture. Think about Danny Zuko (played by John Travolta) in the 1978 musical *Grease* when his friends ask if Sandy Olsson (Olivia Newton-John) 'put up a fight', or just about anything that Glenn

Quagmire does in *Family Guy*, including leaving a woman tied up in his basement. Even more recent shows like *Game of Thrones* depict sexual assault repeatedly – some estimates put it north of 50 times. We also normalise male sexual entitlement. In 2011's *Crazy, Stupid, Love* a boy repeatedly tries to force his babysitter to go out with him – even though she has already turned him down – culminating in a very public proposal. This is not too dissimilar from Ryan Gosling's character Noah Calhoun in *The Notebook*, who threatens to jump off a Ferris wheel if Rachel McAdams character (Allie Hamilton) doesn't agree to date him. Music videos are no different: it wasn't that long ago we saw Robin Thicke and Pharrell Williams' video *Blurred Lines* with its lyrics (and visuals) that seemed to endorse non-consensual sex. Williams later said he was 'embarrassed' by the song.

Our culture also pushes heteronormativity – the assumption that everyone is heterosexual. This is a major theme of many popular reality programmes like *Love Island* or *Love Is Blind*, with producers saying that including people of other sexualities would present 'logistical difficulties'. Heteronormativity is part of the Man Box and something that men should subscribe to in order to be proper men. It is sold to us everywhere, from reality shows to *Disney* cartoons. Queer characters when they do appear on screen are frequently tokenistic, plot devices or seen as appealing to a niche audience, although this is improving. Another similar romantic notion we are sold is the 'happily ever after' – the poster romance, the childhood sweethearts, two halves of a love heart necklace. And these norms aren't just on screen, on billboards or posters, where we might expect adverts. This selling is woven throughout our culture, a never-ending feedback loop.

In sports, many female athletes in the public eye are required to be more sexualised than male counterparts – often to make money for advertisers, appeal to sponsors or fans. In 2021, at the European Beach Handball Championships, the Norwegian women's beach handball team was fined £1,296 for wearing shorts instead of bikini bottoms by the European Handball Federation (EHF). Male players can wear a tank top and shorts while women must wear the bikini with a 'close fit and cut on an upward angle towards the top of the leg'. The rules see women's discomfort, or women being turned off from the sport altogether, as secondary to the need to sell the idea of these women as sexual as well as sporty. At the Tokyo Olympics, also in 2021, the German women's gymnastics team unveiled long-legged unitards in a stand against 'sexualisation'.* It was 2018 before walk-on girls were removed from TV darts competitions, reversing the long-established practice of

---

* There has been an ongoing conversation about whether airlines should be allowed to require female flight attendants to wear make-up and heels on board. Norwegian Air made headlines in 2019 after it emerged that it reportedly required flight attendants to carry a doctor's note if they wanted to wear flat shoes. The airline revised the policy. Our culture is still primarily concerned with how a woman's clothing looks, not how it functions – you only need to ask any woman who has ever been overjoyed to find working pockets (rather than a fake seam that gives an illusion of pockets) on an item of clothing.

beautiful women escorting male players to the stage. Like dominos falling, this was swiftly followed by Formula 1 bosses removing grid girls. The women were generally responsible for holding umbrellas or name boards, lining corridors, wearing branded merchandise and popping champagne. The women did not race, have jobs within teams or even speak in most instances. Defenders of practices like grid girls often advocate choice feminism, saying that women should be allowed to make money in this way if they choose to. However, you'd be hard-pressed to argue that using women as aesthetic furniture, whether in newspapers or on medal podiums, doesn't send a message to both young women and men about a woman's position in the world.

As well as setting the bar for behaviours and norms, through culture we are constantly being sold masculinity and femininity, male sexual entitlement and sexualisation of women to make money for brands. We know sex sells – we only need to look at a 2009 Burger King advert for its seven-inch sandwich in Singapore with the caption 'it'll blow your mind away', a picture of an open-mouthed woman looking shocked, eyes bulging, as the sandwich comes towards her ready to be rammed down her throat, a blatant example of sexualising women. Or the 2015 Protein World advert picturing a woman in a bikini with the caption: 'Are you beach body ready?', which capitalised on stereotypes of the idealised sexy woman to sell workout supplements. Or a 2019 ad by a Nottingham air-conditioning supplier that pictured a woman in denim shorts with the slogan: 'Your wife is hot, better get the air conditioning fixed', which succeeds in both sexualising the woman, removing her agency to do her own DIY and bestowing the role of fixer to a man (not pictured). Research into adverts by Unilever in 2016 found 90 per cent of women felt presented as sex symbols in adverts while 30 per cent said adverts only showed women as perceived by men. The same study revealed just 3 per cent of adverts ever featured women in a managerial or professional role.

In advertising, companies long used the motif 'shrink it and pink it' (i.e. make it smaller and in the colour pink) in marketing products to women. Yes, it sounds like it's from a *Mad Men* script and it has been argued this would not fly in a boardroom pitch now, but we don't have to look far to find examples where products are clearly being marketed in gendered ways. If you go into any toy shop across the UK, you will see toys clearly delineated by gender. Stacks of pink bicycles towering opposite blue ones. Let Toys Be Toys, a campaign to stop marketing products as gendered, has an annual silliness awards, where it highlights the worst examples. In 2021, this included a 'Disney Princess Working Mum' gift set – 'shows that nothing is safe from pinkification' – a pink globe and lunchboxes with the labels 'girls' treasures (something pink and fluffy)' and 'boys' stuff (space stuff, secret weapon)'. But this doesn't stop with children. Products are marketed to adult women this way too. In 2009, Dell launched a new laptop for women that could be used to find recipes online, watch online fitness videos and – of course – track calories. Don't forget the infamous 2012 Bic lady pens, labelled as 'For Her' in an array of pastel colours, or the Pritt Stick glue in pink with the caption 'Just 4 Girls'. In 2018, the CEO of PepsiCo was criticised after saying the company was trying to develop a range of crisps for women that fitted in a handbag and crunched less loudly when eaten.

Just as products are marketed to women, we cannot forget about the exploitation of masculinity (keeping men firmly in that Man Box) to grow sales. What other reason could there have been for Kleenex to brand its extra-large tissues as 'man size' for decades? Describing them as 'staying strong when wet'. Or Nestle's Yorkie chunky chocolate bar that long advertised itself as 'It's not for girls'. Products are siloed into being for men, gatekeeping with colours or names products that are fundamentally the same as women's (although women still pay a 'Pink Tax' on toiletries like razors, frequently in saccharine colours, while men are given a neutral colour on the same product). When selling men products like skincare, historically seen as a gendered purchase for women, companies try to counteract that legacy with overtly masculine messaging. Take Bulldog Skincare with the tag 'We understand men' and a photo of a British Bulldog. Skincare generally falls into the same territory as candles when being sold to men – available in 'masculine' scents like tobacco, leather, dark rum or ash (those are all real).

Boys are not exempt from gendered selling. Clarks labelled their children's school shoes with the descriptors 'Leader' and

'Dolly Babe' respectively – I'll leave you to guess which was which. Some adverts do acknowledge the absurdity of the masculine stereotypes but still, ultimately, rely on them. Even if in a tongue-in-cheek way. In the mid-noughties Lynx adverts, the deodorant caused women in bikinis to flock towards men. This might have been a parody, but it was parodying what is expected of men – to be hypersexual and wanting the attention of women. A 2003 Super Bowl advert for Miller Lite beer, 'Miller Lite Girls', which showed two women arguing, then fighting, mud-wrestling and finally kissing, was framed as a spoof of a male fantasy but the brand was accused of trying to circumvent accusations of sexism by turning it into a joke. Ultimately, the aim was still to get male attention and sell beer.

Crass clichés of sexism are less tolerated in advertising these days, particularly with social media giving consumers a direct hotline to voice disapproval, but culture is resistant to wholesale change. Consider that when brands have attempted to move the dial on what masculinity could look like, we see backlash. When singer-songwriter Harry Styles appeared on the cover of *British Vogue* in a dress, despite skirt and high-heel wearing originating with men riding horses, and everyone from Henry VIII to Roman gladiators wearing the equivalent of modern-day skirts, right-wing commentators lamented the 'steady feminisation of our men'.*

---

* Fashion historians have noted how pink was considered a boy's colour in the eighteenth century because it related to red, interpreted as aggressive and passionate.

Or when Gillette tried to flip its classic 'The Best A Man Can Get' advert to 'The Best Men Can Be', showing the hardships men face and how men could adapt, some claimed they would never buy Gillette again, that it was 'feminist propaganda' and 'absurd virtue-signalling PC guff' (that one was journalist Piers Morgan).

Subversion of supposed masculine norms is seen as firmly in the realm of counter or fringe culture. As well as wanting our culture to reflect dominant masculinity, we also see protest when women are given different roles. When actor Jodie Whittaker was named as the new Doctor Who, there was weeks of coverage documenting the uproar, with some viewers unable to comprehend that an extra-terrestrial Time Lord could have a vagina. There have been many similar discussions around a new James Bond in the 007 franchise.

In other areas brands have attempted to use progressive ideas, or at least the veil of them, but are not really challenging the narrative. A 2020 poster by a SEO (search engine optimisation) provider was banned by the advertising watchdog ASA after using the phrase: 'You do the Girl Boss thing' to advertise its services. In fact, feminism has become a selling point for brands in recent years. International Women's Day is the hotbed of commercialised feminism under the guise of empowerment – a feminist Christmas, if you will. Like clockwork we see discount vibrators, slogan T-shirts, fake tan, boob mugs and teeth-whitening sets appear on the shelves. Fast fashion clothing brand I Saw It First even took the date in 2022 as a chance to flog free anti-spiking drink test kits with every order, while Pretty Little Thing went for a website banner that read 'My dress doesn't mean yes'. Even porn behemoth Pornhub has been known to change its logo to include the internationally recognised female symbol for 24 hours.

Prior to shutting its doors, Topshop was another brand keen to join the commodification of feminism to get the cash registers flying. One of the best examples was its £18 block letter 'FEMINIST' T-shirt that many argued was likely not empowering the women tasked with producing it en masse in factories around the world. It felt even less sincere when a year later, in 2018, author Scarlett Curtis revealed a pop-up stand to promote feminism in the Oxford Street Topshop store was dismantled after 20 minutes over a disagreement with Sir Philip Green. Topshop apologised and decided to donate £25,000 to a charity instead. Meanwhile other brands and organisations take International Women's Day as an opportunity to ask women to speak on panels for free or create viral social media campaigns. In March 2022, Twitter account the Gender Pay Gap Bot took the liberty of retweeting IWD campaigns of companies with the often humiliating pay gap information of that firm. Yet more evidence that feminism is just one of the latest convenient ways of trying to sell to women, rather than a real indication of change inside.

Since the turn of the century we have seen a move away from brazen celebration of British lad culture and adverts that are quite so explicitly sexualising: an end to the era of *Nuts* magazine and

FHM, although *LADbible* is still going strong as a media force to be reckoned with, and commitments by big brands like Unilever to consider sexism when devising commercials – no longer always having a woman hoovering or cooking for her family, or a man being useless at childcare. In 2019 a new advertising rule, set by the advertising watchdog, ASA, in the UK banned harmful gender stereotypes in ads that means they must not include 'stereotypes likely to cause harm, or serious or widespread offence'.

But we still see sexism. Even the UK government fell foul in 2021 and was forced to pull a Covid 'Stay Home, Save Lives' advert depicting all chores being done by women. The lone man was reclining on a sofa. And in a globalised world, it is easy to be exposed to adverts from elsewhere in the world without the ASA rule. In February 2020, KFC in Australia released an advert of a woman in a low-cut top pushing up her breasts as she looked at her reflection in a car window. Two boys are ogling her. The young woman says: 'Did someone say KFC?' The backlash was so swift that the fast food chain promptly issued an apology. Brands do see the ramifications of criticism: in 2019, a Peloton advert depicted a woman grateful to her husband gifting her an exercise bike. The criticism of the advert knocked the value of the company by a reported £1.1bn.

Although we are seeing brands more aware than ever that the outright objectification and sexualisation of women will not be tolerated by consumers, our consumer culture is still nowhere near detached from damaging gender stereotypes. The notion that some companies knowingly take the risk of a bad advert going viral, riding the rollercoaster of outrage, being chewed up and spat out by social media, before inevitably pulling the ad often feels a possibility, under the old umbrella of all publicity is good publicity.

And as we've seen, this isn't just about what happens during the ad break or in a sponsored Instagram post, it's also about our wider culture and how it sells gender stereotypes to us. Our media, our films, our television programmes, our books, our music. And of course social media websites like TikTok are the new frontiers in advertising and culture. It is yet to be fully seen whether we will see a disruption of gender stereotypes on these platforms, or users looking to build quick followings resort to the same techniques as traditional media.

Despite advertisers being gradually forced away from the overt sexism of previous decades, the industry does still only reflect how fast it thinks society is moving. Feminism and the empowerment of women only became a billboard-friendly subject once it was deemed palatable enough so as to be unconfrontational. And Man Box masculinities, as we have discussed already in this book, have a firm grip on the reins of power. Sticking to the old rules is monitored by both our peers and our culture. As men begin to look at the parts of masculinity that might not be serving them, or might be actively harmful to women, they also need to consider how culture and advertising are one of the ways these ideas are being reinforced. But beginning to acknowledge there are alternatives out there does put a chink in its armour.

In the last few chapters we have begun to unpick how inequalities proliferate across different arms of society, how each wing can strengthen the patriarchy in its own way through setting cultural, historical or economic norms of inequality, but how do we further this as individuals? Let's examine how interpersonal relationships and the assumptions we make about women can extend the sphere of patriarchy's influence even further. And ultimately set the stage for violence.

8

Look Beyond Consent

'Hey, would you like a cup of tea?' A cartoon stickman on a white background is putting the kettle on and wants to know if you'd like some. It's a fairly unconventional way to begin a discussion about sexual consent, but in 2015 this was the approach taken by Thames Valley Police in their Consent Is Everything campaign. The two-minute sketch video, which has been watched on YouTube over 10 million times, continues with this tea-making act in different scenarios. 'If they're unconscious, don't make them tea. Okay, maybe they were conscious when you asked them and they said yes, but in the time it took you to boil that kettle, brew the tea and add the milk they are now unconscious. You should just put the tea down…' it goes on. 'If someone said "yes" to tea at your house last Saturday that doesn't mean they want you to make them tea all the time or to wake up to find you pouring tea down their throat.'

Getting to a stage where we now mostly agree on the necessity of securing consent is no small feat. It is set against a cultural background that sees a prince saving a princess from an enchanted sleep with a kiss, as a fairy tale for children. Even though *Sleeping Beauty* is very much asleep, the story of a stranger's kiss is told as romantic, not perhaps as being a little inappropriate. Elsewhere, brands like Dolce & Gabbana have made adverts accused of 'simulating gang rape', with a group of men surrounding a woman lying on her back on the floor to sell luxury clothes – the advert was pulled – and beer companies have had to apologise after encouraging customers to 'remove "no" from your vocabulary for the night'. Teen films like *American Pie* (1999) have also portrayed teenage boys trying to livestream sex with an oblivious exchange student as funny after-school hijinx, not voyeuristic or potentially criminal.

The past decade has seen an uptick in public conversations about consent – and actively getting it before a sexual interaction – in response to the #MeToo movement, greater coverage of rapes on US college campuses, and the general volume of women's negative experiences now given voice and platform by social media. This is a positive step and not one to be overlooked, but in understanding power dynamics, and dynamics of inequality, in interpersonal (heterosexual) relationships we must go beyond just considering consent. Not least because relying on just getting a simple yes or no as confirmation of an all-round positive experience is a house of cards waiting to crumble. Just because someone said yes, that doesn't mean the sex was enjoyable, was without pain or trauma, was not bad, that it fulfilled their needs or that they entered into it for any reason than feeling like they *should*. Consent is easily conflated with they-didn't-explicitly-say-no type logic, or a murmured submission of yes over unmistakable enthusiasm and can be too reductionist (consider the scrapped Good2Go app, one example of tech that asked both parties to tick a pre-sex consent box). We must step back to look at the bigger picture. Because it's not really about sex, it's about power.

We have seen how other areas of our lives – culture, laws, language – are the beams that give strength and structure to the subordination of women and consequently violence. But we have spent less time examining how this plays out in interpersonal relationships. As feminist Carol Hanisch said, the personal is political, meaning the things we experience as individuals are rooted in systems. Our personal actions help perpetuate systems of inequality.

This chapter will look at our understanding of gender roles in relationships, in sex, the acquisition of pleasure and the impact of porn. I want to go beyond a simple question of consent and see how misogyny, power imbalances, entitlement, the leverage and misuse of political inequality between men and women applies in the bedroom. How we should be trying to develop our understanding rather than flatten it for simplicity. How all of these things matter when we ask questions like – why didn't she just get up and leave? If we cast our minds back to Chapter 2 when we looked at the Aziz Ansari case we noted that we should not gloss over such uncomfortable examples but ask why men and women could come away with such different feelings. Having nuance is crucial as men begin to interrogate their behaviour to achieve a future where violence against women is not an inevitability for so many.

In an article published in *The Week*, journalist Lili Loofbourow vocalises a disconnect she sees at the heart of the Ansari case: that, in general, men tend to use the term 'bad sex' to describe a boring experience, a passive partner, or at worst, a lack of orgasm. When women talk about 'bad sex', they mean something totally different – coercion, emotional or physical discomfort and pain, which they are conditioned to sit with, or ignore, rather than vocalise (for fear of hurting men's feelings or bruising their egos). Michaela Coel's BBC series *I May Destroy You*, released in 2020, adeptly tackled the variety of experiences that can sit within the big tent of bad sex. The show was based on Coel's own life and asks a central question about whether we can pigeon-hole our experiences of bad sex into something that 'counts' as bad *enough*, sometimes having to suppress our feelings of discomfort and trauma because they don't neatly match textbook rapes or assaults. Writing in *The Cut*, Sangeeta Singh-Kurtz says: 'I know many people who have had similar experiences, and have used similar language to describe them: It wasn't bad; it wasn't good; I don't remember much; probably not again; did I want it? I'm not sure. It was weird. A vague script.' But just because an interaction isn't criminal, just because it is *technically* consensual, it doesn't mean it is not sexist. It doesn't make it a positive experience.

Pain during sex is common for women. Studies vary on how many women experience pain during sex: some say it is one in every 13 women, other research shows up to 30 per cent of women have pain with vaginal sex, 72 per cent during anal sex. And large numbers do not tell their partner. As well as physical pain, heterosexual women are most likely to be denied pleasure. They are victims of the orgasm gap. Studies have shown they are the least likely to experience orgasms during intimacy, with heterosexual men most likely to say they always orgasmed during sexual intimacy (95 per cent), followed by gay men (89 per cent), bisexual men (88 per cent), lesbian women (86 per cent), bisexual women (66 per cent) and finally, heterosexual women (65 per cent). And men aren't even necessarily aware of this; research cited by the Kinsey Institute found 85 per cent of men reported their partner had an orgasm at the most recent sexual event, compared to 64 per cent of women who reported doing so.

Women's pain and lack of pleasure might seem totally inconsequential when compared to violence, but it speaks to the same underlying assumptions that men's needs come ahead of women's needs. Heterosexual sex is still primarily about male pleasure and desire and women being as accommodating as possible in achieving that goal. Just as we've seen other parts of society that focus on the centrality and power of men. But why do we still see sex this way?

We are told that men are the sexed gender. Men are expected to want sex all the time, to be thinking about sex every seven seconds. Sex is classified as a need for men, like oxygen or sleep. Think about the deployment of the term 'blue balls' to pathologise the need to orgasm – if women deny this to men it becomes a medical emergency. If women express overt sexual desire in a way that is seen as threatening to men as the sexed gender then they are categorised as nymphomaniac – a word that literally can only apply to women (the equivalent for men is satyromania, but how frequently is that term deployed?). In Nora Ephron's *When Harry Met Sally*, Harry declares: 'No man can be friends with a woman that he finds attractive. He always wants to have sex with her.' Dan Guinness, from Beyond Equality, tells me that masculinity has a central role in teaching men how to behave: 'I'm both talking about a lot of pressure to be straight and to be visibly active or visibly [sexually] successful. To have lots of nudes on your phone and show them to your mates.' Although we see an ever-greater expression of women's sexuality in our culture, it is still often for the male gaze.

Indeed, Dr Fiona Vera-Gray says we should look at how heterosexuality positions men and women. Men are perceived as out acting in the world, where they are given space, and are making things happen (we've seen this in our history and culture) while women have things happen to them. The perception of men as eternally on the hunt, while women lie back and think of England, lingers on. We can see this both in our perceptions of heterosexual sex – language and understandings of virginity and it being something that is 'taken' from passive women by active men and has a cultural value and power to possess it – and in expressions of romance and commitment. In the UK it is still uncommon for a woman to propose to a man. One survey found that in 2010, 5 per cent of women proposed and in 2019, it was 16 per cent. Although an increase, still hardly the norm. Men still make things happen.

Guinness says although things can seem like small considerations when looking at violence, when you actually unpack them 'they're all around objectification of someone else, projection of your own desires without recognising or creating space for someone else to have agency, and a lack of empathy'. And we see feelings of male sexual entitlement crop up all over the place: men seeing women as trophies to be won or men referring to being kept in the 'friendzone' as an admission of failure. The friendzone only exists when male entitlement to women's bodies in return for emotional closeness is an accepted part of masculinity. In the absence of male entitlement, the friendzone ceases to exist. Andrea Simon, director of the End Violence Against Women Coalition (EVAW), says from a young age we see boys winning masculinity kudos from other boys for treating girls in harmful ways, like getting them to send sexual photos that are then frequently shared among peers. During a 2021 Ofsted investigation, school inspectors were told boys shared nude pictures of girls on apps like WhatsApp and Snapchat 'like a collection game'.

It is this intersection of sexual prowess as an indicator of masculinity, and male entitlement through patriarchy, that is dangerous. Of course some men are never going to ask for consent – content with knowingly raping a woman for their own agenda. But there are plenty of men who could be perpetuating harm by failing to see the entitlement and power imbalance that sets the standard for their sexual behaviour. When expectations are fuelled by entitlement (i.e. I want sex so we should have it) and motivated by the compelling idea that securing sex confers masculinity, asking for consent can feel superfluous. Men are coming to those interactions already feeling it is something they deserve to have and something women are obligated to give. It is seen as implicitly available, on the table, unless a woman is explicitly screaming no. A 2018 YouGov and EVAW study found a third of men think if a woman has flirted on a date, it generally wouldn't count as rape, even if the woman has not agreed to sex. These would-be rapists, who likely do not see themself as such, highlight the flaw in depending on active consent conversations as a catch-all safety net. If men feel entitled to women's bodies asking for consent is often going to feel surplus to requirements.

On top of the standard package of male entitlement, we can add further layers such as when money is involved. This of course applies to the purchase of sex that can often involve violence used against those selling it, but also to dating scenarios. A 2010 study titled 'You Owe Me' looked at perceptions of rape after a date when different people had paid for a date. It found male respondents believed that when a man had paid entirely for an expensive date, both the man and woman should have expected sex. When the cost of a less expensive date was split, no sexual expectations were owed. As a result, if a sexual assault had occurred after the cost of a date was split, the perpetrator was assigned the most blame rather than feeling that the victim had some responsibility because they'd accepted the meal. We see this transactional view of sex in the Netflix series *Maid*, about a mother, Alex, who attempts to leave her partner, Sean, taking their two-year-old daughter. Another male character, Nate, offers to help Alex with a car and somewhere to sleep with no strings attached, but kicks her out when she repeatedly rejects his romantic advances. We see how entitlement (for sex or female attention) isn't just as a result of forcefulness or dominance but can also surface when men think they've been nice enough, or spent enough, to deserve it.

It would be impossible to examine our modern sex lives without also considering the question of pornography and what it teaches us about how men and women should interact and their expectations of each other. Debates over the power of porn have long seen lines drawn in feminist discourse – with some arguing that porn depicts and therefore helps normalise women's subordination (feminist and professor of law Catharine MacKinnon described it as '[a] message addressed directly to the penis, delivered through an erection, and taken out on women in the real world'), while others insisted that porn was an extension of women's sexual liberation and an expression of pleasure. Today, one thing is clear: the scope of porn's influence is bigger than ever before.

TechRadar reports that adult website Pornhub is one of the two most heavily visited websites in the US, receiving an average of 639 million monthly visitors and outranking Netflix and Zoom. Professor Clare McGlynn talks about this prevalence: '[Porn] is so ubiquitous it can't not impact on everything. I'm not saying you use this material and go out and commit a sexual offence, [but] it is literally the background wallpaper to our culture because millions are watching the stuff.' Of course there are feminist porn directors, like Erika Lust, producing a different type of sex-positive porn, but we cannot pretend that this is what the majority of porn users are watching when vast digital warehouses of free porn are available at the touch of a button.

Rachel Thompson, journalist and author of *Rough*, tells me that there is a particular concern about young people learning sexual scripts and norms from porn against a wider context of poor sex education in the UK. 'They think that is a realistic representation of the sex that they'll have, the lack of consent negotiation that takes place…spontaneous sex, use of choking and BDSM acts incorporated without consent protocols,' she says. 'What we're talking about is misinformation and misrepresentation of the reality of sex, and when you mix that with pretty abysmal sex education, it's a recipe for disaster.' In a BBC survey of people aged 18–25 in 2019, 55 per cent of men and 34 per cent of women said porn was their main source of sex-ed. Andrea Simon, director of EVAW, told me that she is concerned about young people 'particularly [those] who haven't even had any sexual experience themselves': '[They are] access-ing pornography and seeing that as a standard and it sets so many expectations around what sex is. We've heard accounts of boys saying, "Yes, she was crying, but I thought that's what girls like because that's what I've seen."'

As well as sexual scripts, lots of porn reinforces social scripts that sees women resisting sex, being inexperienced or virginal, trying things for the first time, always having to be coerced by the man (or men) until they finally say yes – a cat and mouse game that is fetishised. Women are already conditioned in all other aspects of life to put everyone else's comfort ahead of their own; these scripts both capitalise on and reinforce that.

Not only is porn relevant here because it is filling a void of sex education, but in the era of internet porn, sexually violent material is no longer hidden on a top shelf or in niche places where it has to be sought out. Nor is it restricted to a BDSM context (with relevant safeguarding). Studies have found violence is promoted to first-time visitors on the landing pages of the UK's most popular porn websites. Over a six-month period, a team at Durham University analysed 150,000 video titles and found one in eight described sexually violent, coercive or non-consensual content. This includes criminal acts like rape, upskirting and incest, and others like hair pulling or spitting. Many of the examples of porn video titles are so graphic in nature that they have to be censored when being submitted for reports to Parliament, says Professor Clare McGlynn. Women have also extensively reported the non-consensual upload of private videos and the battles with porn giants to have them removed.

Depictions of violence do not always remain a fictional fantasy, we're seeing porn-learnt behaviours filtering through to the sheets. On paper there is nothing objectionable about adults expanding their sexual repertoire by watching porn. It can be a way to learn about kinks or sexual preferences, but it does become an issue when behaviours are taken out of context, such as BDSM without safeguarding, when they become an anticipated part of all sex, when people feel shamed for being 'vanilla' if they are not interested, or when things are just simply non-consensual. A third of UK women under the age of 40 have experienced unwanted slapping, choking, gagging or spitting during consensual sex, research for BBC Radio 5 Live suggested. Thompson shared an example of a heterosexual couple who engaged in regular choking but had never actually discussed it – when the man felt emboldened to ask his partner why she liked it, the woman confessed she hated it and was only doing so because she thought he wanted it. We can also see porn impacting what young people want to try in sex. A 2016 report on young people by the Children's Commissioner found a greater proportion of boys wanted to emulate what they see in porn than girls.

Although exposure to porn does not directly cause non-consensual violence, it does create a climate in which violence and violent acts, like slapping, can move more seamlessly from the screen to the bedroom, particularly for young people learning sexual scripts from a screen who have no other frame of reference. To acknowledge this is not hand-wringing or a moral panic but recognising that the mainstream pornographic landscape is not automatically advancing women's sexual liberation. It has not stripped away stigma and given women licence to self-pleasure without shame (a staple theme of much porn is 'slut-shaming'). Actor Rashida Jones, who directed Netflix's documentary, *Hot Girls Wanted*, about the amateur porn industry, made this distinction: '[There is a] difference between [expressing] sexuality and sexualisation.' The feminist sexual revolution will not be made by Pornhub.

We don't need to be anti-porn as a general concept to recognise that the current mainstream offering is problematic for its focus on the sexualisation of women as vessels to be at the disposal of men, the excessive violence (without any BDSM protocols or contexts), total heteronormativity and perpetuation of racial stereotypes.

Porn also helps to feed masculinity stereotypes that we are looking to combat – particularly the virility myth. Or the idea that 'real men' are always up for sex. Rachel Thompson says this is the idea that men have 'huge throbbing penises, are always dominant, always ready for sex, take the lead, the woman is submissive…that idea permeates into society and makes men think they don't have the right to say no to sex,' she explains. 'Research shows these gender roles lead men to consent to sex that they don't want to have because they think [men] should always be up for it. It can violate their own boundaries.' In an episode of *Friends,* Joey and Chandler find a porn channel and refuse to turn it off, despite wanting to: 'Then we'd be the guys who turned off free porn,' they protest, suggesting it would undermine their status as men and even fathers. Joey says: 'I want to have a kid someday and someday that kid is going to ask me if I ever turned off free porn, I don't want to have to tell him that I did!' Although this is comedy, it shows how the Man Box pushes men to adopt certain sexual habits. Thompson says if we could stop ingesting ideas about masculinity and virility it could improve the sex we have and help us question the sex we feel obliged to have.

From September 2021 a new sex and relationships education curriculum is being taught in UK schools. It is now compulsory and will cover everything from consent and sexual images to coercion and victim blaming in age-appropriate ways. But the limitations of it are already becoming apparent. Journalist Sophia Smith Galer writes in her book *Losing It* that when she filed a Freedom of Information Request to find out how many times the training module had been downloaded by teachers it was way off the mark. By October 2021, only 1,775 downloads had happened. There are 3,456 secondary schools in the UK, not counting independent senior schools. In a separate report, the school standards minister admitted there had been no training in four out of five schools. There is clearly a long way to go.

For adults who have long been out of a school setting – how do we begin to do the work? – Dr Fiona Vera-Gray says people should try to stop watching porn: 'Understand that you are going to have to stop doing some of the things that are enjoyable for you. To actually change [the system], we need to give up a bit of whatever we're doing that is complicit or participating' – especially when no one else is looking because that is when we all buy into patriarchy. Sociologist Michael Flood says that fundamentally we have to accept that in shifting norms around sex, men will have to give up benefits they might have previously enjoyed. 'If we can make significant progress towards ending men's sexual violence, then I can no longer assume then that when I want sex, we will have sex, I can no longer assume that my sexual needs and my sexual desires come first, I'll have to actually negotiate consent and respect my partner's wishes. But, I'd say that it's only fair that men let go of these unearned privileges.'

Sexual violence, or violence in relationships, is ostensibly a huge part of gender-based VAWG. It is crucial for men to see how sexual entitlement means it's not just a handful of 'bad apples' who need to sit up and listen, but something that everyone should consider. We must realise that consent is too low a bar when battling against unacknowledged feelings of entitlement and male power that are only aggravated by learning sexual and social scripts from porn while inclusive and honest sex education remains somewhat elusive.

Many of the previous chapters have focused on overarching structural inequalities that, while crucial to understand, are harder to set about transforming single-handedly. But interpersonal relationships are an arena in which men can start to see how gender inequality is reinforced day-to-day and how far they are compliant in that. Have men ever engaged in non-consensual sex? Pressured women into something or left a woman in pain? Believed that their right to orgasm was the only thing that mattered? Is the porn that men are watching showing violent acts without any consent or the constant humiliation and shaming of women? Bad sex might seem like a frivolous concern but it speaks volumes about the underlying assumptions we make about men and women – who matters, who acts and who submits. We must challenge this culture of sexual and social entitlement that is the fuel on the fire of gender-based violence.

As we move into the final part of the book we are going to start looking at how men can practically step up and be counted – the things they should be doing, the things to avoid and how best to motivate men to do this work over a period of time. As we've discussed already this isn't just about talking directly to those who are violent – it's about all men. Confronting the norms that facilitate gender-based abuse within a patriarchy and challenging harms even when they stray uncomfortably close to home.

9

Challenge Your Assumptions

A man and his son have been involved in a terrible car accident and are rushed to the nearest hospital A&E department. The boy needs surgery but the doctor takes one look at him lying on the trolley and says: 'I can't operate on this boy, he's my son!' How could this be? Answer: The doctor is the boy's mum. If you've been anywhere near the British school system or a playground in the last 50 years you have likely heard this hackneyed riddle – or an iteration of it. It is silly and few people probably don't know the answer by now (sorry for the spoiler if so), but the fact that it has stayed the course for quite so long does tell us something about the subconscious assumptions we make. Even in twenty-first-century Britain, the fact that a woman as a surgeon could be a mind-boggling punchline really doesn't show us in the best light.

Earlier in the book we spent time confronting our assumptions about men's violence, those who are capable of doing it and those who are not, but now it is time to dig deeper and look at how our assumptions about women are the scaffolding that help to prop up and sustain men's violence. Even if men are not perpetrators themselves, the things they might believe about women nourish a system in which it requires 60 women to secure a conviction against actor Bill Cosby (his sexual assault conviction was overturned in 2021 after he served two years in prison, he was then released); more than 80 against former film producer Harvey Weinstein, who was sentenced to 23 years in prison in 2020 for rape and sexual assault, and two decades of allegations to convict R&B singer R. Kelly on charges of sex trafficking (it is worth noting that these women were Black, compounding false assumptions about credibility). Why is one woman's voice not enough? Why are women not seen as universal truth tellers?

While men are seen as neutral and objective – the ground zero for experiences from which everything else deviates – women are often seen as emotional or hysterical, a word that originates from the Greek word for uterus, *hystera*. Adult women have been diagnosed with hysteria as far back as the ancient Egyptians, who wrote about the condition on papyrus. Conveniently, it was claimed that the condition was resolved by sex, through the healing properties of semen. Laughable as that may be, the perception of women as prone to hysteria has persisted from the Salem witch trials in the late 1600s to former PM David Cameron telling Labour's Angela Eagle to 'calm down, dear'. When women express strong emotions in a meeting at work it is because they are unable to control themselves; when men do the same it is because the circumstances require it, they are passionate and in control (unless they are a Black man, then they are dangerous and out of control). It might seem inconsequential to think of your female colleague as emotionally fragile in a meeting about budget reports, but it is one of many stones that cause ripples in the deep and treacherous waters of inequality. Because casually dismissing women as overly-emotional – also, read 'shrill' – allows us to not believe them and to resign their feelings and lived experiences to being irrational and, crucially, false.

Society has long made assumptions about women's fallibility. Women are not even trusted as witnesses to their own pain. Researchers have found when male and female patients express the same amount of pain, observers view the female patient's pain as less intense and more likely to benefit from psychotherapy versus medication. This is even greater for women of colour and other minority women: Black women are four times more likely to die in childbirth than their white counterparts in the UK because of their concerns being dismissed or ignored and denial of pain relief due to racial stereotyping. In Abby Norman's book *Ask Me About My Uterus* documenting her endometriosis journey, she was dismissed by doctors until she went to an appointment with her then-boyfriend, who vouched for her pain (saying it was impacting their sex life). The doctor then acted. 'Becoming a disappointment to a man seemed to do the trick,' she writes. In the UK, despite endometriosis impacting one in

10 women of a reproductive age, around 1.5 million women, according to support network Endometriosis UK, on average it still takes eight years for a diagnosis to be made. This bias about women's liability to error is informed by a historical lack of medical research on women compared to men, as well as assumptions about truth telling.

This type of assumption seeps into how seriously women are taken about everything, but particularly when discussing men's behaviour. New York's *Daily News* parodied the propensity to say things like 'it's a he said, she said case' with the headline: 'He said, she said, she said, she said, she said, she said, she said, she said [cont]' about the Bill Cosby case. But not taking women's word for it can have fatally dangerous consequences. Retired Detective Superintendent Caroline Goode shared a story as part of the Femicide Census, in which she explained how not believing women can, in some cases, end in their death. 'For me, the most tragic murders of all are those where the victim has sought help and not been believed,' she says. In 2009, Goode investigated the murder of an elderly Jewish woman, a Holocaust survivor: 'The woman had told police that men were living in her basement. She was dismissed as delusional. In fact, two men had broken into her basement. They tied her up and tortured her, leaving her to die of exposure over Christmas.' In another case, Goode dealt with a Kurdish woman who was eventually killed by her family after approaching the police five times seeking help: '[She was] dismissed as melodramatic.'

In 2015, *ProRepublica* published an investigation that would later be turned into a Netflix series, *Unbelievable*. The show, based on true events, charts the story of Marie, 18, who was raped at knife point by a man who broke into her flat in Washington, USA. After making an initial police report, various people – including Marie's foster mum – started to suspect that she had perhaps made up the rape. This deduction was based on Marie's behaviour, which they deemed not fitting of the circumstances. As a result, Marie was hounded by the police into recounting her story over and over again, pulling out small inconsistencies each time. She felt pressured to say she lied originally and the police charged her with filing a false report. Eventually Marie was able to receive justice for her rape, but only once her story had been corroborated by a number of stories from fellow survivors, who were targeted while the perpetrator remained at large because Marie was not believed.

Clearly such a story is shocking and we'd like to think it's a complete rarity, but it is not. In 2016, Shana Grice, 19, from East Sussex had her throat slit by her ex-boyfriend after a long stalking campaign. Michael Lane had broken into Shana's house and watched her sleep (she was actually awake), fitted tracking devices to her car and called her to breathe heavily down the phone from withheld numbers. Shana had reported his stalking to the police but instead of being given help she was handed a £90 fixed-penalty notice for wasting police time. Shana had even recorded evidence of the phone calls to give to officers. Sussex

Police later revealed 13 other women, not including Shana, had also reported Lane for stalking. In the case of John Worboys, the black cab rapist who was handed two life sentences in 2009, one victim, 19, claimed that when she reported her story to police they 'laughed' and did not believe her.

These stories straddle a crossroads of common assumptions about women. The first is preconceived notions about how female victims should act when making reports – putting women on trial – and the second is the bogeyman of the false accusation. This has, for a long time, been seen as a tool utilised by vengeful or mentally unstable women for their own gain. The spectre of the false rape accusation is one that hangs on, in spite of all evidence that demonstrates such cases are rare. In 2013, the Crown Prosecution Service (CPS) published a report looking into the phenomenon and showed that over a 17-month period there were a total of 5,651 prosecutions for rape and in the same period, 35 prosecutions for false allegations of rape. This is 0.62 per cent. Even among that small number, the CPS concluded 'in some cases, the person alleged to have made the false report had undoubtedly been the victim of some kind of offence, even if not the one which he or she had reported'. What is far more likely than false accusations, according to the stats, is that women won't be believed when they are telling the truth. In 2014, a joint government-police monitoring report indicated a 'culture of disbelief' as police forces wrote off up to a third of all rape allegations reported to them.

Even if women are believed when they first make a report, they then have to jump through hoops all the way to court. Reporting by *Vice* exposed how women were regularly being told not to access therapy until after their trial – endangering their mental health in the process – in a bid to make them the most credible witness if they took the stand and to avoid accusations of being 'coached' in their story. In 2012, the head of the Crown Prosecution Service (CPS), Alison Saunders, even confessed that she knew women were not coming forward to prosecute rapists because they – the victims – feared being demonised by the jurors. Jamie Klingler, a co-founder of Reclaim These Streets, described women as having 'a trial in [our] own mind': 'We've gotten to a point societally, where if we are sexually violated our thought process is – is this prosecutable? Rather than us dealing and processing the fact that we were violated, we are like "would a jury believe me because of how much I had to drink?"'

Home Office data from 2021 showed 41 per cent of rape victims and survivors are 'withdrawing their support for action' during the criminal justice process (up from 25 per cent in 2015–16). Evidence of these problems was so widespread that in June 2021 the UK government made a commitment for a £3.2 million police pilot, named Operation Soteria (Soteria being the Greek goddess of salvation), to focus investigations on suspects rather than the complainant's credibility in future.

These tactics play against women, who – because of our societal assumptions – simultaneously have to prove they are damaged enough to be believable, but sufficiently in control that they have not imagined or daydreamed this horror. And some women have to work even harder to be believed, particularly women of colour, or women made vulnerable by factors like living in poverty. The inquiry into the Rotherham grooming scandal – which saw the abuse of girls as young as 11 between 1999 and 2013 – found that police and council workers had referred to child victims' abuse and rape as 'lifestyle choices'. In 2014, Valerie Forde and her one-year-old daughter Jahzara were murdered by Valerie's ex-partner. Six weeks earlier, Forde had told police that he'd threatened to burn down her house with her in it. It was recorded as a threat to property, not a threat to Forde's life. Her murder has led to petitions calling for police to be trained in dealing with Black victims of domestic abuse and their specific cultural needs.

Assumptions also lead to a so-called hierarchy of victims. A pretty, white, middle-class woman out for a run is often positioned as a 'less deserving' victim – 'she did everything right,' we chime – than say a sex worker, a migrant woman or a mother who stayed living with her abuser for decades. Like the Victorian deserving and undeserving poor, or the good and bad migrant. Although such sentiments help articulate the feeling of raw helplessness post-tragedy, it provides a feedback loop to sustain ideas about women's behaviour correlating to harm. Feminist author Laura Bates wrote on Instagram in 2022: 'It plays into this insidious narrative of the perfect victim who deserves our sympathy and grief because she did everything right when we say that, no matter how unintentional, there's a tiny unsaid implication that some women do deserve it.' Newspapers also still use headlines that suggest women incited harm, such as: 'Strangled wife had taunted husband's bedroom prowess'. The Femicide Census found media examples of all the following reasons being given for a woman's death: leaving the perpetrator, beginning a new relationship, having an abortion, using alcohol or substances, asserting herself, being involved in sex work, having a 'chaotic life', being naive or difficult.

While the bar for women to be believed is high, the bar for erring on the side of caution to protect men can be desperately low. In the film *Promising Young Woman* (2020), we see the college dean tell Cassie: 'What would you have me do? Ruin a young man's life every time we had an accusation like this? I have to give him the benefit of the doubt.' This has been described by author Kate Manne as 'himpathy', when we worry about a man's future being ruined above and beyond worrying about the impact of violence on the female victims.

Women have to contend with excuses being used as explanations for their victimhood – being drunk, being mentally ill – but the same excuses are wheeled out in the defence of men (unless you are a Black man or other ethnic minority). Anthony Williams, 70, who strangled his wife to death, was cleared of her murder in February 2021 and jailed for five years for manslaughter on the grounds of diminished responsibility, claiming he was depressed and anxious during the Covid lockdown. In the US, Brock Turner was convicted on three charges after sexually assaulting Chanel Miller at Stanford University. The judge Aaron Persky sentenced him to six months, of which he served three, arguing that he considered Turner was 'intoxicated at the time of the incident'. In his statement, the judge said: 'It's not an excuse, but it is a factor. And I think it is a factor that, when trying to assess moral culpability in this situation, is mitigating.' Assumptions lead to a double standard in which women are more responsible for what happens to them when they drink, while men are less.

There is a reason defence lawyers still try to use the 'nagging and shagging' defence on jurors when defending men accused of harming women. The defence implies that the woman either hassled a man sufficiently, denied him sex or had sex with someone else, causing the man to retaliate violently. There is also the 'rough sex' defence. Although a law in England and Wales now rules out consent for sexual gratification as a defence, and a victim's sexual history can no longer be routinely heard in court, we still see it in practice. In September 2021, a man who strangled a woman after drinking 24 bottles of beer was given less than five years in prison. Sam Pybus argued he had not meant to hurt Sophie Moss, 33, during 'consensual rough sex'. The defence is still used to discredit women, even those who can no longer speak for themselves. Elsewhere in the world we've seen gratuitous examples: in the New Zealand trial of Grace Millane's killer, it was argued that her death was a result of a 'sex game gone wrong', citing her preference for

BDSM-style sex as justification. The 2018 Belfast rape trial of a group of Irish rugby players saw a bloodied lace thong passed around the courtroom and jurors asked to consider her choice of underwear. The men were found not guilty.

Women's clothing has long been a source of assumption-making, an explanation for the fate that befalls them. A Sky News presenter, Stephen Dixon, prompted anger in 2017 during a debate about women in skirts, saying: 'Is it a dreadful thing to say that if women are out in short skirts and drunk that they don't need to take any personal responsibility?' While women are 'asking for it' in short skirts, they are simultaneously told that they are 'unrapeable' in fitted clothing – in 2010 a man in Australia was acquitted of rape after a jury found the victim could not have been raped while wearing skinny jeans because they would have 'required collaboration' to take off. In a 2021 *Tortoise* media podcast, *Hidden Homicides*, Professor Jane Monckton Smith, a former police officer and criminologist, said: 'All of these defences are sitting there boxed ready to go. You can almost go to the shelf and say right, we're going to use the "wearing a short skirt one" and everyone just goes along with it.'

Even the language that forms the building blocks of legislation designed to protect women makes assumptions about them. In 2015, the Revenge Porn law was introduced in England and Wales that makes the sharing (or threatening to share) of private, sexual materials of another person illegal. This is if it is without their consent and with the purpose of causing embarrassment or distress. But the name of the law has been criticised. 'The word porn makes it sound commercialised, like we want this,' victim-survivor Lauren Evans told me when I interviewed her in 2019. 'The definition of revenge is someone doing something to you because you've done something to them – it implies the victim must have done something to deserve this.' She, and another campaigners, says image-based sexual abuse would be a more fitting definition that does not carry unspoken implications about the women who have been victimised – that they deserved it or caused it to happen.

Although such victim-blaming can sound extreme and many men would not identify with it, it can still be connected to our everyday treatment of, and assumptions about, women's ability to recount the truth. Are men always listening to women and accepting their interpretation of events at face value without presuming hyperbole, sensitivity or melodramatics? This line of thinking isn't just when listening to women tell stories of violence or harassment, but in daily conversation. A 2018 study from Arizona State University found men overestimate their own intelligence and credentials and underestimate the abilities of female colleagues. If men consistently presume the women around them are less knowledgeable or smart, we can see how this feeds into men second-guessing much of what women are saying. Particularly if it is on a topic the man is less familiar with, or might feel threatened by.

Men should be aware of this if they find themselves taking everything women say with a pinch of salt, feeling they need to corroborate what she says either with another man, or with an external source – like Google or Wikipedia. Again, this can be about mundane subjects, general knowledge, or trivia, not just stories of violence or sexism. It might particularly be the case if the topic is something traditionally seen as 'male-interest' like sport, economics, politics, gaming or technology. And if it is something the man feels he should have known but did not. If a woman has taught you something new, be aware of any compulsion to feel one must cross-reference that, either right in front of her or at a later point. If women are never seen as trustworthy sources or given credence on even the most basic of topics, we can see how this leads to the undermining, or outright dismissal, of their voices when the stakes are higher. Particularly if men are then confronted with two opposing accounts from a woman and a man (add in if this is a man held in high esteem or respected).

Men should also be wary of biases they have when interpreting how a woman has dealt with a situation – are they quick to jump to seeing a woman as more emotional or 'highly strung' than if a man had behaved in the same way? Would they interpret however the man had reacted as proportionate to the situation instead? This can be seen when terms such as 'feisty' or 'bossy' are used to describe women but would never be used for a man even if he reacted in exactly the same way. Such gender bias is not acceptable, and men should work on identifying it and changing it within their own minds, but it is also a result of a system of inequality. To soak up some of the sexist messaging we are surrounded by every day is not an indictment of total failure or abject bad character. But to see it, ignore it and refuse to change this is a different matter entirely. Men should also be aware that they can still be vulnerable to making assumptions about women as a gender, even if there are some women one holds in high esteem or respect. This is where we might hear phrases such as 'you are not like other women' – men should learn to praise or critique women without demonising other women in the process. 'You are not like other girls' is not the compliment a man might think it is.

Systemic assumptions are evidently harder for an individual to wake up one morning and set about changing, but we are not exempt from having these assumptions taint our worldview. It is a deep-rooted misogyny that means men do not trust what women are telling them. It is more convenient to believe she has an agenda, that she is perhaps a raging feminist or has a political motivation. This can partly be in a bid to protect the status quo; for anyone it is confronting to hear that what we thought was the truth is not. There is a phenomenon known as identity-protective cognition in which individuals who encounter new information that threatens their beliefs tend to dismiss it. Like a reflex. In this sense it is more threatening to men's sense of self that women are telling the truth than are wrong.

Furthermore, hearing that women have been harmed can threaten men who feel pressure to live up to the protector role assigned them by the Man Box. It is disappointing for these men to feel they were unable to do more, both because of guilt around their manhood and sadness for the women who have been harmed. In short, it is convenient to not take seriously what women are saying a lot of the time because it involves introspection. But countering this begins with empathy and listening. Accepting that just because a man hasn't borne witness to something, or doesn't know something, doesn't mean it cannot possibly be true.

Most of us are not members of the police, responsible for taking reports from women who have endured trauma, or members of the judiciary – sometimes perhaps part of a jury tasked with making such a decision – but this doesn't mean assumptions don't have consequences. We not only need men to start listening to women, we need men to start believing what women say. Men fundamentally need to believe that what women are telling them matters.

10

Do Not Push Out Women

'The petticoat no longer makes the suffragette. We are suffragettes – suffragettes in trousers.' Those were the words of Israel Zangwill, member of the Men's League for Women's Suffrage, in the early 1900s. There have long been small bands of men who have worked as co-conspirators to advance women's causes. In 1907, the Men's League for Women's Suffrage was founded, followed by the Men's Political Union for Women's Enfranchisement in 1910. Labour MP George Lansbury was one of the best-known male supporters of the call for women's suffrage after he gave up his seat in the House of Commons in protest against the treatment of female prisoners. He was briefly imprisoned for a pro-suffrage speech at the Royal Albert Hall. Other liberals and radicals supported suffrage, including playwright Laurence Housman, Reverend Claude Hinscliff (who campaigned for the ordination of women after the war) and Frederick Pethick-Lawrence who, with his wife Emmeline Pethick-Lawrence (Pethick was her maiden name, they added it to Frederick's surname when they married in 1901; they also kept separate bank accounts), provided their home as the HQ for the Women's Social and Political Union and played an active part in the militant suffragette movement between 1906 and 1912.

In the early 1900s, Labour MP Keir Hardie often raised the women's vote and the plight of imprisoned suffragettes in Parliament, and Millicent Fawcett's husband, Henry, provided financial support for the cause. A group of Scottish councillors named themselves the 'Men From The North' and travelled to Westminster in 1913 to pressure the government further. 'To fight for the women—our only desire,' they wrote in a song enroute. Philosopher Bertrand Russell argued in his 'Liberalism and Women's Suffrage' article (1908) that 'no man can call himself a democrat if he is in favour of excluding half the nation for participation in public affairs'. In 1908, Victor Storr and Thomas Bayard Simmonds threw suffrage leaflets from the public gallery in the House of Commons, which set in motion the so-called Grille Protest that saw women chain themselves to the screen in the Ladies' Gallery in the Palace of Westminster. Henry Selfridge used the suffragette colours in his department store windows on Oxford Street (it helped that he wanted them as customers). Evidence also exists of working-class men in the Edwardian period going on hunger strike, publishing suffrage material and supporting pressure groups for the cause.

During the second wave of feminism, known as the Women's Lib (or Women's Liberation Movement) from the 1960s to 1980s, feminists called for social, sexual and reproductive liberation for the sisterhood. Men were again a part of the early movement – Nicholas Owen wrote in *Men And The 1970s British Women's Liberation Movement* that men were present at the first national conference at Ruskin College, Oxford, in February 1970 (a man even made the final speech on the second day) and around 25 per cent of those at a demonstration in March 1971 were men. Men's childcare initiatives also developed – staffing crèches at meetings and events, sociologist Stuart Hall was one of those manning the crèche at Ruskin – and the first Men Against Sexism conference was held in 1973. But this period also saw many WLM groups closed to men and deep fault-lines develop over the issue of men's inclusion. Women were keen not to rely on men to speak for them and there began to be much greater scepticism of men's motivations.

As we break down the places for men to start, we should also note the things they must avoid. One of the biggest tensions in involving men, historically, is the risks it presents to the women already doing the work. These include, but are not limited to: men being given more credit for reiterating women's ideas (the long-documented 'pedestal effect'); bad actors using it as a way to whitewash their own behaviour without consequence; diverting already minimal funding from women's groups; men being given a greater platform or brownie points for such work; men claiming expertise in areas they do not have for recognition and a fundamental replication of the same patriarchal inequalities we see everywhere else, with women's voices being drowned out by men who feel they deserve to lead. Indeed, Dr Burrell says it is 'very easy [for men] to go out there as a white knight, we've got all the answers and can solve this'.

During the second wave these concerns were foregrounded in the organisational process, with a schism in the WLM movement born over the man question. For socialist feminists it made sense to include men, given they were also part of the wider pushback against capitalist forces that included the oppression of women, there was already a precedent of organising alongside men, and alienating them might be an unnecessary way of removing potential allies. But for radical feminists, on the other side of this splinter, involving men risked replicating the same gendered problems they had seen in the rest of society. As time passed, certain events didn't help dissuade the sceptics. At the Skegness conference in October 1971, a male speaker refused to give up the microphone to women; men wrote in to the women's groups frustrated at not being included by women and the men's group retained a female typist for their newsletter.

In her *Dreams and Dilemmas: Collected Writings* (1983), Sheila Rowbotham wrote: 'The most obvious block to us is the difficulty that men have, no matter of what revolutionary persuasion, in learning anything from women'. One male supporter, David Ratovitsky, noticed this for himself in a mixed-sex support group: 'Listening is very difficult for many men; we are not used to doing it. In fact, most of us are so unused to listening to women that we don't even realise we're not doing it.' This also presented old tensions of whether women should be responsible for educating, nurturing and spoon-feeding men while they underwent processes of consciousness-raising.

In the London's WLM newsletter, *The Shrew*, Hilary Rawlings wrote that women had seen men's support as 'always conditional'. More women began to withdraw and focus on separatism as a goal – some even advocated for political lesbianism to cut all ties with men. By this point, Owen writes that 'men's groups seemed to show too little progress to justify the price of readmission. Some were reasserting their masculinity in a manner which came close to an anti-feminist backlash. Others had not fully appreciated the extent of their privileges or were unwilling to give them up.' Even those men who had achieved some degree of transformation veered towards being too introspective, wallowing in guilt or shame, and remained too fearful of confronting other men – something we will discuss in a future chapter.

These risks are not old news, they are still with us. A piece of research from 2021, titled 'Men's Activism To End Violence Against Women: Voices From Spain, Sweden and the UK', gave an example of a man in the UK in this field who had 'unrealistic' expectations of women's groups he wanted to work with who had not replied to an email he sent: 'He explained the lack of reply as being because he was a man and that the women's organisation would not want to work with him on the basis of his sex. However, the women's organisation in question is under-resourced, overworked, with serious life-threatening cases of male violence, and it is likely that many researchers' emails go unanswered regardless of the sex of the researcher'. The researchers say that it seemed like the man had 'expected a certain "pedestal" status' that he did not get and failed to understand the pressures such an organisation might be facing. Karen Ingala Smith, founder of the Femicide Census, has also written about 25 November becoming known globally as White Ribbon Day – a men's anti-violence campaign – that now overshadows the International Day for the Elimination of Violence Against Women that already existed on the same date. It is noteworthy that the day was created in honour of three women of colour – the Mirabal sisters who were assassinated in the Dominican Republic in 1960.

This battle of the sexes approach, the classic *Men Are From Mars, Women Are From Venus*, calls to mind the words sung by fictional suffragette Mrs Winifred Banks in Disney's *Mary Poppins* (1964): 'Though we adore men individually, we agree that as a group they're rather stupid'. The risks of involving men in women's liberation have long been recognised and continue to be real, but there is also a danger of polarising positions, entrenching would-be supporters, isolating some women and feeding populist anti-feminist rhetoric on the right. As feminist author bell hooks wrote, keeping men out 'helped to marginalise feminist struggle', making it seem a personal solution to individual problems rather than framing it as a 'political movement which aims to transform society as a whole'. This is particularly true, hooks says, in reference to the disconnect that many women of colour felt. How many of these women struggling against racism alongside men of colour would choose to be separated from them? And for all women, how realistic is separatism, particularly in financial terms?

'We need to have more of a discussion and be clearer about what the risks are so that we can deal with [them] rather than kind of write off [men's involvement] as it can't happen because of the risks,' says Professor Nicole Westmarland, director of the Durham Centre for Research into Violence and Abuse. 'Even with "good men" we see them saying things which have been said many years before by feminists and not taken seriously and getting a round of applause for it.' With these risks, and a legacy of divisions in mind, it is crucial for men embarking on this journey to get rid of any preconceived chivalric notions or saviour complexes. Women do not need rescuing nor are they asking for men to come along and validate their efforts with a male stamp of approval. Men should not anticipate being centred in doing this work. The requirement might be more of a backseat position than many are accustomed to.

Furthermore men should be acutely aware of the danger of pushing out female voices, particularly because research has frequently shown us that men's perception of how much they are talking compared to the women around them often skews against women. In February 2021, Yoshiro Mori, leader of the Tokyo Olympics organising committee, stepped down after he was quoted as saying: 'If we increase the number of female board members, we have to make sure their speaking time is restricted somewhat, they have difficulty finishing [talking], which is annoying.'

Mori might have been sexist, but he isn't alone in believing that women talk far more than they actually do. Studies of work and public settings (rather than private conversations) show that men speak more. An analysis of 100 public meetings by the Victoria University of Wellington in New Zealand showed that on average men asked three quarters of the questions even when audiences were equally split. Sue Montgomery, a city councillor from Montreal, Canada, went viral after sharing her piece knitted during council meetings – she used a colour code to denote when men or women were speaking. She knitted in red when men spoke and green for women: the resulting scarf was red with thin patches of green. This was despite the balance of men and women on the council being almost equal (31 women, 34 men).

Even when women do speak, they are perceived differently to men. One 2012 study by a psychologist at Yale University found that when male executives spoke, more often they were seen as competent, whereas female executives were seen as less competent the more they spoke. A 2014 study from the George Washington University in DC, found both men and women interrupted women more than when they were speaking to a man.

As well as being spoken over, women experience having others take credit for their ideas. The annual McKinsey Women in the Workplace report of over 300 companies and nearly 70,000 employees found in 2019 that half of women had experienced being interrupted or spoken over (the number was higher among LGBTQ+ women and those with disabilities) and 38 per cent had others take credit for their ideas. A cartoon published in *Punch* magazine in 1988 parodied this problem. It featured five men and a woman sitting around a boardroom table. The caption was: 'That's an excellent suggestion, Miss Triggs. Perhaps one of the men here would like to make it'. Women have attempted to develop strategies to combat this. In 2016, it was reported that female White House staff in the Obama administration were using 'amplification' to hammer across the points of women that were dismissed. If a woman offered an idea in a meeting that went unacknowledged, another woman would repeat it and give her colleague credit. This repetition meant that eventually the staffer's idea was more likely to be heard, but such strategies still notably rely on women supporting women rather than men just listening.

Not hearing women can also lead to a practice described as 'mansplaining' – a pejorative term where a man explains something to a woman in a condescending and patronising manner (if you're worried you are doing this, ask yourself did she ask for this information, or is it unsolicited, are you making assumptions about her competence or lack of knowledge on this topic, and is it possible this woman actually already knows more about this than you?). Dr Burrell says: 'Listening more to women goes against dominant ideas of masculinity, because listening means placating yourself in that [male-female] dynamic.'

Dr Vera-Gray says tackling this as men begin this journey of learning will be a tension for many. 'How do you speak without speaking over, or speaking for [women]? Be aware that as a man you are going to be invited to speak more and given more of a platform.' Remembering not to push out women is crucial – a first step should be listening to women around you and being informed by what they are telling you, rather than using it as an opportunity for a soap box or to play devil's advocate. And note that listening to women is not the same as asking them to do all the heavy lifting in educating you on this topic.

Men should be alive to the many risks that their involvement presents for women who are extending an olive branch and how they adapt their behaviour to address this. As Simone de Beauvoir succinctly wrote: 'Assuredly, [getting] women's autonomy, even if it spares men a good number of problems, will also deny them many conveniences.' Like the convenience of always knowing you are welcome to talk and lead. Sociologist Michael Flood says you should be aware of how labour is divided when going about supporting women: 'Who is in front of the microphone? Who is setting up the work? Who is baking the cakes? Who is getting the attention?' This involves not competing for funding with women's groups – who are already frequently under-resourced and have been subject to extensive cuts.

Welcoming men to this movement brings both reasons for optimism and reasons for that optimism to be cautious. Previous examples have shown how the inequalities we see elsewhere in

society – and are trying to combat – can just risk being replicated. This particularly means male voices being given platforms
over the voices of women (especially in a field such as this, where
they have a certain novelty factor) and men being given more
credence for ideas that have already been shared by women. There
is an emphasis here on men ensuring partnership and accountability and looking at the work women are already doing. Being
complementary to women's work, rather than ploughing ahead
with your own ambitions without checking in. Women do not
need men's misguided paternalism or hero complex. They need
men to listen, and to hear what they are saying, without feeling
the need to speak for them.

11

Practical Interventions

Getting men to be part of modern solution-building is not completely reinventing the wheel. As we saw in the previous chapter, there is a precedent. The groundwork has been laid. In 2014, *Harry Potter* actor Emma Watson appeared at the United Nations to launch her HeForShe campaign. Watson asked: 'How can we affect change in the world when only half of it is invited or feel welcome to participate in the conversation? Men – I would like to take this opportunity to extend your formal invitation. Gender equality is your issue too.' HeForShe subsequently crashed the UN website more than once, is a term registered in the Urban Dictionary and has had 49,000 signups from men across the UK. The same year, the Obama administration launched an initiative called 'It's On Us' in response to sexual assault at colleges. In October 2021, Women's Aid launched its All Men video campaign, encouraging men to be upstanders, and a group of British male celebrities, including Michael Sheen and Gary Neville, called for misogyny to be a hate crime.

As well as campaigns, there are long-running and well-established men's anti-violence groups like White Ribbon, founded in Canada in 1991, following the 1989 École Polytechnique massacre of female students. Its mission is to end male violence against women and it encourages men to wear a white ribbon and take a pledge to never commit, excuse or remain silent about violence against women. Elsewhere, MenEngage works as a global alliance promoting gender and social justice. In the UK, Beyond Equality (which began as two projects: Great Men and Good Lad) runs workshops for men to attend on rethinking masculinity.

In the weeks after Sarah Everard's death in March 2021, Beyond Equality saw a surge in signups for volunteers. From just four per month, on average, to 74 in a single month and hundreds over the space of a few months. This is encouraging, but there still remains a difference in the number of men signing up and those actually turning up to the sessions. Those who are attracted to the idea of the work in the moment versus showing up at a later date to do it. Nazir Afzal, former chief crown prosecutor for north-west England, told the *Guardian* that in 2016 he tried to organise a 'million man march' and got just 52 signups. In fact, such is the continued scarcity of men in this field that they have been referred to as 'male unicorns'. Although there have been a number of men working diligently for decades, what we need to see now is this shift from a marginal concern to something broader in scope. So how can individual men begin?

On 9 March 2021, Stuart Edwards, a financial planner from London, tweeted: 'I live less than five minutes from where Sarah Everard went missing. Everyone is on high alert. Aside from giving as much space as possible on quieter streets and keeping your face visible, is there anything else men can reasonably do to reduce the anxiety/spook factor?' The tweet was liked and retweeted thousands of times and hundreds of women commented, sharing things they would like to see men do more of.

These suggestions ranged from men crossing the road if you find yourself walking behind a lone woman, to not running close to women or approaching at speed (especially at night); offering to walk female friends home; being noisy if you're walking alone at night behind a woman so you don't appear to be trying to creep up on her, especially if she is wearing headphones so is less likely to hear you straight away; overtaking with sufficient space; not getting into lifts with a lone woman; not forcing a woman into the road by refusing to concede on a small path; and not forcing women to walk between a split group of men on a pavement.

For men such a list of explicit tips might seem helpful in the short term, but it is important not to be lured in by reductive schemes as being all that is needed. Giving men a notebook of rules can be easily forgettable or confused and fails to address the infinite number of circumstances a man might find himself in. We don't want men just waiting to be handed a strict list of dos and don'ts. This can become a suffocating mandate that really only sets us all up to fail or mis-step and done only to win the approval of women or to avoid their critique.

Instead of fixating on decreed commandments, I would hope this book has shown men how to develop a critical understanding of why women might have made these particular suggestions in response to Edwards' tweet. The thread that runs through all of them is having an awareness that women are experiencing that scenario differently to a man. Just because a man knows that he presents no physical threat, consider that a woman's lived experience gives them legitimate reason to be fearful – particularly at night, in the dark, if a man is alone, and adapt behaviour accordingly. Men must develop agency (this does not mean ignoring women if they have suggestions) in thinking innovatively about how to tackle this alongside women instead of relying on a tick-box list that really only gives men a multitude of ways to mess up, rather than a world of opportunities to succeed. Let's consider more broadly useful themes that men can carry forward and use to feel empowered to make their own decisions. This is when it has the potential to be transformative life-long learning. But where to start?

When any of us ask how we can help we can secretly harbour a hope there will be a quick and simple way to achieve our goals. To make ourselves feel good without a huge commitment. To a degree this is human nature. It is similarly tempting to hope that short-term and simple interventions will be able to overnight shift lifelong habits, entrenched inequalities and systemic imbalances.

It would be nice if this was the case, but clearly it will take a little more work than that. There is no silver bullet that women have been concealing from men for centuries, testing them to find the right answer. As we have explored throughout the book, this is about wider changes – beyond a one-day workshop. As Aja Barber, fashion consultant and writer, says in Gina Martin's book *Be the Change*, ally is a verb, not a noun – allyship is something you should be doing in perpetuity, not just a label you choose to wear when it suits you.

Having said that, we should not feel immobilised by pessimism or the size of the hill left to climb. Sociologist Michael Flood says there are all sorts of ways men can start to make a difference: 'It's not that they need to abandon their day jobs or suddenly become a full-time activist, there's all kinds of things that men can do.'

Start close to home

This work always has to start close to home. We live in a time when big gestures (that can be photographed or shared online) and visible action are often seen as the only components of change. A sort of pics-or-it-didn't-happen approach. American politician Alexandria Ocasio-Cortez described this as being wary of 'get rich quick thinking' that only thinks of change in dramatic, sudden and visible shifts. 'The fact is that couldn't be further from the truth. Revolutionary and transformative changes, from the inside out, happen more like mosaics,' she adds. Each small fragment added gradually, to create a pattern that can be replicated and added to. Indeed, for men it is important to begin in your own backyard, with real introspection.

As we examined in earlier chapters, doing the work of starting with yourself is about understanding the extent of the violence problem, about not othering perpetrators or distancing yourself from it. Be the change you want to see. The most useful thing is for all men to see how they might have been a part of perpetuating harm. For the small everyday – laughing along or staying silent as they told sexist jokes – to the bigger harms. And this isn't just about outright violence but about seeing how women are not treated as equal in so many spheres. This is a pyramid of harm and the sharpest end could not exist without the foundational levels. Including asking whether the share of labour in the home is being equally divided. Or excuses drawn up – 'I'd only do it wrong anyway and you'd have to redo it' – to get yourself out of doing that work. Have assumptions ever been made about who would be a primary caregiver, or judgements been cast about women's emotions or responses to situations that you would not have applied to a man?

Starting at the bottom means that we do not swoop in with the minimum commitment to change and attempt to paper over the cracks that really require the whole house to be razed to the ground. This is not a one-off event, a Saturday morning job that is done once and complete. It is not a destination you arrive at and then just sit in, a longer project of reflection and work. Constant reassessment and betterment. We are trying to rewrite society, the way we are expected to behave, and our children are socialised to be. Dr Vera-Gray says: 'We need [men] to start feeling empathy for what it is like to be a woman.' Can you begin to put yourself in a woman's shoes and see how experiences that men might not see as problematic (like commenting on a woman's appearance in the street) are experienced differently because of the different obstacles and experiences women carry?

This self-reflection can, and should, include reading feminist literature (think of writers like Audre Lorde, bell hooks and Maya Angelou) that brings women's voices into your learning rather than letting your own assumptions form the basis of change; signing up to mailing lists such as White Ribbon or Beyond Equality for regular updates and prompts to continue; or listening to podcasts like *Now and Men* for more in-depth discussions about the issues. All of these actions should not be used to supplement introspection or to avoid feelings of discomfort about past behaviour but to facilitate this process.

Listen and speak to women

This work should be led by women – if you find yourself telling women how to move forward or demanding that women make space for you, then you're likely not in the right place. This isn't about coming in and solving the problem for women and pushing them out in the process. Nor is it about taking the focus off survivor stories and spotlighting men. This includes very literal examples of centring men rather than women. When I visited the Clapham Common bandstand after the death of Sarah Everard I was dismayed to see examples of men pushing in front of sobbing women or taking photographs and videos of women visibly grieving. Consider why this might not have been the most appropriate response, even if the right sentiment of support was there. There is a way to show support without pushing out women in the process.

Listening to women is a crucial action in itself, primarily because we still see men struggling to understand women's experiences. This is something that cannot be short-cut around or circumnavigated. If you don't want to hear women, you're going to remain at the start line. We frequently see men still don't appreciate even the basic scale of this problem: a piece of research by Police Scotland in 2021 found men are still widely off the mark when it comes to understanding how women experience harassment. Three quarters of women said groping or grabbing was a regular experience for them, but only a quarter of men thought it was common. Only half of men thought cat-calling was frequent but three quarters of women said it was.

Listening will help men gain a better understanding of these issues. And if women tell you that your actions are not helping, be mindful and take that feedback on board. These conversations aren't always going to happen in a context that you might want either: it could be difficult to navigate because, as we've already explored, women can legitimately be suspicious of men and the risks they present when entering these spaces. But this process of learning shouldn't be centred on confrontation and conflict – where possible, there should be room for nurturing, accountability and active collaboration rather than unhelpful gender siloes.

Move past shame

This work is nothing without being fully accountable and honest about where you've acted poorly. It is a foundational brick in the wall and without it, your allyship is insincere to those you encounter and disrespectful to those you've harmed in the past. But accountability does not mean wallowing in guilt or shame, unable to move past that junction. You need to work through this emotion, which can also cause defensiveness, and channel these emotions into a response.

One man involved in the Women's Liberation Movement in the 1970s found guilt so debilitating that he couldn't even look women in the eye. He told Cambridge University researcher, Lucy Delap, in 2012: 'I remember once being on a tube and reading *Spare Rib* [a WLM magazine] and a woman sitting next to me smiled at me, so I shut my eyes and I kept my eyes shut for the rest of my journey 'cos I just didn't know, I had no idea how to deal with that.' Recently, I had a conversation with a male friend who told me he sometimes feels like he wants to speak up and do more, to call out friends when he thinks they're acting inappropriately, but is incapacitated by his own history. By sexist ways he behaved as a teenager, phrases he used and how he spoke about (and to) his girlfriend at that time. Shame can be a powerful motivator but it can also be like quicksand: easy to get stuck and sink early in. It does not always foster action.

Go beyond tweeting – educate yourself

As with most social justice issues, it is obvious that sometimes those looking to do the right thing slip into performative or tokenistic allyship. The effort to demonstrate that learning is taking place behind the scenes becomes the end goal, rather than learning as a means to change. Remember, this isn't just about what you post on Twitter. The women in men's lives do not need them to use hashtags or post photographs of vigils if they are still having sexist conversations with their friends or controlling their girlfriend.

Jasmine Mohammad works for the Angelou Centre in Newcastle, which provides holistic support for Black, minoritised and migrant survivors of domestic and sexual violence. Mohammad says that she often sees men posting on social media about this but thinks they might be better off focusing elsewhere: 'I've seen a lot of things posted saying, "We should be doing this, we should be doing that", and I always think that it's important you're expressing your views, but actually doing that work privately is really important. Education, reading, speaking to women close to you.'

Social media can help in distilling complex issues and problems into more easily digestible chunks – this increases accessibility and knowledge (as long as the information is correct). But often the material becomes so flattened by the requirements of social media to be clickable, likeable, shareable that it omits or loses nuance. This is where people must treat learning online as a launch pad rather than the be-all and end-all. Men should make sure their education is not just for optics and it is something they are motivated to change for their own reasons. This is when we will see ongoing and sustained change rather than a flash in the pan.

Adopt a personal language

As we've already established, one of the best ways to make this a long-term change (because this will be a process, not an overnight fix) is to develop a personal language that makes sense. This includes men asking why they care and why they want to do this work. What is incentivising you to change? This will be useful when thinking about moving beyond education just for the sake of being seen to do the right thing. Sociologist Michael Flood says developing a personal language could stem from hearing the story of a particular woman, or making links between women's experiences of violence and the violence you have suffered, or other forms of social disadvantage like racism or homophobia: 'Whatever that language looks like, men need to develop a way of speaking from the heart,' he says.

Christopher Flux from the Men Against Violence group in Preston tells me over email that men, like anyone doing work on themselves, can often struggle for lack of time due to other commitments like work and family, so we sometimes have to find ways around that: 'We all have different skills, resources and our own individual sphere of influence,' he says. 'I try to meet guys where they are at and individualise the approach depending on the audience.' Flux worked with an Imam and a biker gang on different projects – 'A teenage male goth, for example, might respond to something differently than a middle-aged football fan or an elderly Muslim, a socialist man might frame violence against women as an "equality" issue, whilst a conservative might see domestic abuse as an affront to "family values".' The aim, he says, is not to make everyone a dedicated feminist but to help men be an ally, no matter what situation they're in.

In making this a long-term change, we cannot hope that a cookie-cutter-one-size-fits-all response is going to inspire all men; instead we must try meeting them where they're at. This is about framing the same core message in the way that makes most sense to each man. Is the man doing this to help his wife, sister or girlfriend, or because he is finding masculinity limiting on parts of his personality? Is it because he has experienced male violence and wants to reduce it? Or simply because he thinks it's the right thing to do? For men, understanding what is the underlying motivation will help when times are testing.

Don't leave women out

Making groundswell change under a banner of social justice is nothing if it leaves out the very people who need it most – if we only work for the advancement of the least-marginalised women, which can happen when only doing the absolute minimum required. In this context that particularly means including women of colour, LGBTQ+ women, working-class women, women with disabilities, trans women and others who are dealing with intersectional forms of violence (the term coined by Kimberlé Crenshaw that we discussed in Chapter 1, *see* p. 21).

Mohammad says often 'certain women are completely left out of the conversation' and that men coming to this work must do so with an intersectional lens: 'I think it's really important that men understand that women have different forms of social identity, and that they can interact in a way that creates really distinct forms of oppression and violence,' she says. 'Men should look out for that in the way violence is perpetrated. When you have a Black woman or minority woman that's experiencing sexual harassment that often has a racialised as well as sexualised aspect to it.' This could mean experiencing racist as well as sexist insults.

Intersectionality also changes how violence is reported and responded to. Black women are less likely to get an equitable response when they come forward. Mohammad says: 'So many of the women we have worked with who have reported [violence] to the police, actually have ended up in prison cells for 24 hours because perpetrators have been listened to over victims because of racism, institutional and structural racism, as well as sexism.' When men are looking to be part of this conversation, they must understand how women do not experience sexism and misogyny equally and there are different layers at play that mean a woman might, for example, be more hesitant to report to the police or to seek support. Having an awareness of this is key.

Be innovative

Cristiano Ronaldo's return to Manchester United football club in 2021 was a historic occasion for crowds at Old Trafford. But amid the excitement, feminist group Level Up didn't want fans to forget about the rape allegations made against Ronaldo (which he denies and will not face charges for). On 11 September, the group flew a small plane over the pitch just as the team were kicking off their game against Newcastle. A banner behind the plane read: 'Believe Kathryn Mayorga'. Organiser Janey Starling tells me it was male donors who funded that flight.

Of course, most men do not have enough money to fund a plane, but Starling says it is a good example of men helping where they are needed in pre-existing work: 'It is important [for men] to take the lead from the people, I would ask men to look around and get stuck in where you can,' she says. Starling gave another example of a feminist direct action group occupying the roof of a building in protest against cuts to services. Men in the group drove the van to the back of the building, got the ladder out and held it as the women ran up, then they packed the ladder away, leaving the women to lead the action while the men helped with the logistics in the background. Maya Tutton, co-founder of Our Streets Now, similarly says that men have offered the group free advertising space and have helped draft legal proposals.

For men wondering how they could help in similar ways, why not think about offering free child care at protests? Attending a vigil but making physical space for women rather than yourself? Donating some of your salary to a rape crisis centre without telling anyone? There are so many ways men can help in their own lives and innovation is welcome.

Think about broad changes

Fundamentally, this work is about calling for men to demand change both to the state of sexual violence in the UK and the subordination of women more broadly. This is a structural issue and will require changing society, it is not a simple case of just asking men to stop being violent (although this would help). Long-term change over generations comes by swapping systems, not just relying on individuals to do the right thing.

Think about misogyny built into our systems, like the police. In the five years to 2021, UK police forces received more than 800 allegations of domestic abuse against officers and staff, BBC research found. Just 43 cases, about 5 per cent, were prosecuted.

In 2022, the Met had to apologise and pay compensation to an academic for 'sexist and derogatory' language during a strip-search, including jokes about the smell of the woman's knickers. Another damning investigation by the Independent Office for Police Conduct, released just weeks later, found officers sharing sexist, racist, homophobic messages between 2016 and 2018, including 'I would happily rape you' and 'If I was single, I would happily chloroform you'. Another said: 'Getting a woman into bed is like spreading butter. It can be done with a bit of effort using a credit card, but it's quicker and easier just to use a knife.' The messages continued: 'You ever slapped your missus? … It makes them love you more. Seriously since I did that she won't leave me alone'.

At the end of 2021, two Met constables were jailed for 33 months for taking pictures of murdered sisters Nicole Smallman and Bibaa Henry and sharing them on a WhatsApp group. Even after the death of Sarah Everard, and the attempts by women to show solidarity at Clapham Common, this arm of the state exercised brutality towards unarmed, peaceful women. Women also cited 'intimidation' by police after the vigil had ended. Patsy Stevenson, 28, who was memorably pictured being handcuffed on the floor, said 'about 50' officers had contacted her on dating app Tinder since her arrest, leaving her 'terrified'.

With systems like these – especially those tasked with rooting out injustice – it will always be an uphill battle to make change. This inequality in systems extends well beyond the police when we look at our judiciary, our immigration system and other government bodies.

The government can make policy decisions that directly harm women, such as reversing access to abortion pills by post that made at-home terminations possible during the pandemic (note, the government eventually voted to keep this service). The UK government also decides on legislation that can protect or expose women to greater harm. Calls on the government to make misogyny a hate crime have been approved by the House of Lords but rebuffed by Prime Minister Boris Johnson. Mr Johnson told BBC Breakfast in October 2021, 'If you simply widen the scope of what you ask the police to do, you'll just increase the problem.' A separate criminal offence for public sexual harassment, which had almost 500,000 petition signatories, is still waiting in the wings.

Men should be challenging structural misogyny and sexism as a broader programme of radical work, lending support or voice to legislative change proposed by women and rallying behind those already working in this area.

In this chapter, we have begun to lay out how men can do work on themselves. In picking up and reading this book you've already taken that first step, but it is important to lay out the roadmap for when you've reached the last page. These are broad themes but essential groundwork for all men: examining your own behaviour and where it might be helping to support inequality, listening to and hearing women, developing an understanding of your own motivations, using intersectional analysis and seeing this as part of a larger package of work that needs to be done to change how sexism and misogyny works at a national, and global, level. All of this requires honest introspection and willingness to make change beyond a single tweet or hashtag, but it will also require talking to other men.

12

Call Out Those Around You

A man got in touch with me at the end of 2021 to explain a conundrum he was facing. He was in his late twenties and had recently been out with his girlfriend. They'd walked past a bar together, she was a few steps ahead of him because the path was too narrow to walk side by side. As she passed the bar, the male bouncer on the door spun around and gestured to smack her on the bottom. Unhappy about this, the man – for the first time ever – had decided to verbally confront the bouncer to ask why he'd done that to his girlfriend. In response the bouncer physically assaulted him, pinning him against a fence.

The man was hurt and wanted to contact the bar to report what had happened, but his girlfriend asked him to leave it alone. She explained that she didn't want him to press the issue in case the bouncer was sacked or would recognise her in future and target her. He did as she asked. Despite not taking further action, the man told me that he felt helpless. Spurred on in the wake of high-profile killings of women like Nessa and Everard, he had wanted to start doing more, but after this attempt he felt demoralised and despondent. If a similar situation occurred, he admitted he would walk on, just try to ignore it: 'What now?' he asked.

This story articulates a number of points: first that, as previously mentioned, we can see how violence against men is linked to the same issues facing women and how eradicating men's violence would be mutually beneficial to men and women. Second, we must delve deeper into how men can go beyond themselves to work with other men on this issue, to bring them into the circle of change, and how best to equip them to execute this.

Men must understand that in order to do this work well it does not require jumping into physical altercations or putting oneself in harm's way. Of course if anyone sees a person being harmed, they can take a stand, but long-term, we don't want to just train men to be glorified security guards, vigilantes dispensing 'good-guy' violence. As we've spent a large portion of the book doing, this work needs to be rooted in understanding of social justice and how gender relations are part of wider systems of inequality. We are creating long-term change, not just stepping in and taking the punches on the behalf of women.

In the previous chapter we explored ways men can individually begin to do this work. And while the grass roots movement will begin with individuals stepping up, men will need to bring in others too. The marxist-feminist journal *Red Rag*, published between 1972–80 by members of the Women's Lib [WLM], told men this: 'The WLM is giving notice that it is no longer sufficient politically to be a "liberated" male towards women. What we are looking for now is how male/men relate to other men and to the patriarchal structure in which we both live.' In 1997, South African President Nelson Mandela told a national men's march, 'Until today, the collective voice of these men has never been heard because the issue has not been regarded as one for the whole nation. From today, those who inflict violence on others will know they are being isolated and cannot count on other men to protect them.'

Today, the same is true – men must be ready to work on themselves, as detailed in the previous chapter, and then with those around them. To speak openly about these issues with friends, brothers, sons, fathers, uncles, colleagues and the wider community. But this can be intimidating, so it is useful to understand why we need to bring in others to this learning.

Social experiments – and real-life horror stories – have shown that in situations where strangers are being hurt or need help, too often people walk on by. The 1964 murder of 28-year-old Kitty Genovese in New York was witnessed by 38 neighbours but none came to her aid (one eventually called the police). In 1993, when two-year-old James Bulger was led away from the Bootle shopping centre where he was kidnapped, video evidence showed people watching. Later testimony revealed the number of bystanders was also 38. We frequently don't interrupt, do not play the good samaritan, we let things happen. Often through the (legitimate) fear that the violence we're witnessing might be redirected at us. But this also happens among friends and family. Too often we neglect to act even in low-stakes scenarios, allowing sexist comments or bad behaviour to pass by.

Educator and author Jackson Katz says within groups we know it is not fear of physical consequences but social ones – ostracisation, verbal attacks, bullying, falling outside of the Man Box – i.e. accusations of homophobia, virtue-signalling, betraying your sex, not being a *real man*. Or, quite simply, making the situation awkward. Both peers and culture indirectly police this, ensuring men do not feel empowered to speak up. Katz told me: 'Men are afraid of other men, whether they say it out loud or can articulate it, they're very worried about the opinions of other men, they think they're going to lose status among their male peers or somehow jeopardise their standing with the lads. That is incredibly powerful as a social control mechanism of men.'*

But speaking up matters because 'When [we] don't speak up, that man will leave the conversation or interaction thinking that behaviour was fine,' says sociologist Michael Flood, citing a speech given by Lieutenant-General David Morrison, former chief of the Australian army, in which he said, 'the standard you walk past is the standard you accept'. Whether that is another man telling a sexist joke or having a violent outburst. Not only does men not

---

* The strongest predictor of men's willingness to intervene is their perception of other men's willingness, according to a 2003 study by Patricia Fabiano.

saying anything reinforce to perpetrators that it is acceptable, there are also places and spaces where women will never be invited and so rely on men to have these conversations on their behalf. Male locker room talk is one such example. In 2016, US President Donald Trump defended his 'grab 'em by the pussy' comments (2005), saying it was just 'locker room talk' – implying that it was acceptable because of the context, an all-male space where such conversations happen. It is in these very spaces that we need to do the work rather than only preaching to the converted.

So what can other men do about it? This isn't about men throwing themselves into violence like Superman, but seeing how it is the responsibility of those in groups with privilege to challenge those who abuse that power even in the face of discomfort.

The bystander approach has been used by Jackson Katz since 1993 as part of his pioneering Mentors in Violence Prevention (MVP) programme. Katz, and many feminists I've consulted, have described this as having a ripple effect – seeing all men and women as having the potential to make change on the ground. Instead of focusing on men as only potential perpetrators and women as only potential victims – which struggles to get most men to buy into the idea, as they see themselves as non-perpetrators – it positions everyone as a potential bystander. Everyone has the capacity to change things. The bystander approach began as part of anti-bullying work but was adapted by Katz to use with sports teams in schools, on campuses and later with the military. He tells me it was crucial to work within cultures where ideas about manhood are reproduced: 'If we just stayed on the margins and worked with men who've been harmed by traditional patriarchal hierarchy and violence, the system could go on for decades and centuries. You've got to go into the centre, to the hegemonic and dominant culture,' he explained.

The bystander approach is powerful because of social norms theory. Social norms theory, as written about by consultant Alan Berkowitz, describes situations in which individuals incorrectly perceive the attitudes of their peers and larger community to be at odds with their own, also known as 'pluralistic ignorance'. For example, thinking that everyone at university is drinking more alcohol than you. The problem with this assumption is that the individual then adjusts their behaviour to be in line with what they perceive to be the norm. So they drink more, not less. 'In other words, the majority is silent because it thinks it is a minority, and the minority is vocal because it believes that it represents the majority,' Berkowitz writes. This is important in the context of men's violence because, he adds, 'Men underestimate other men's discomfort with sexist comments and are more willing to confront perpetrators when they believe that other men feel the same way.' The way to break this cycle then is to provide accurate feedback by speaking out instead of going along with what we perceive to be the norm in a race to the bottom.

The bystander approach works by giving men permission to act by recognising that speaking out actually takes a lot of courage rather than being the easy option of a 'weak man' or a 'man betraying his sex' (anyone who has tried will know this difficulty first-hand). Speaking out becomes a quality of leaders in a group, not losers. In this, men should not shy away from being strong – as Man Box masculinity dictates they are – but to channel that strength into moral conviction and speaking up rather than brandishing fists. Over time this change for speaking out to be associated with leadership will hopefully shift the group dynamic so more men want to identify with being outspoken. Framing this action as an aspirational quality for men also moves us away from the idea of only doing this as a temporary favour to women, one that can be conditional, feels entitled to women's unwavering gratitude and is easy to shirk off in spaces away from the eyes of women.

The bystander approach focuses on giving 'a menu of options for intervention' writes Katz, including even those who are not present when violence occurs. 'People needed to know they had numerous nonviolent alternatives to consider beyond the fight, flight, or freeze instincts of our evolutionary inheritance,' he writes. If a man is out with friends and one of them is speaking aggressively towards his girlfriend, it isn't the case that they have two options: a) physically jump in, or b) do nothing. There are a variety of ways the man can try to de-escalate what is happening. Firstly, disrupting the situation – why not try to distract the man by talking loudly about another topic they know he is interested in? Or ask one member of the couple if they'd like to come to the bar to grab a drink. The distraction technique was used to great effect by 24-year-old architect Charles Sonder in 2012 on the New York subway. A video of Sonder went viral after he stepped in between two strangers arguing. He did not try to fight or even say anything to either person, he just stood eating his Pringles (he later became known in the media as 'Snackman'). But it diffused the situation.

If a distraction approach doesn't appeal or doesn't seem right for the situation, men can try an intervention at a later point in time. Take the girlfriend to one side and tell her you noticed what was happening and ask if you can do anything to help. Or confront the friend and say that you thought he should have handled it differently. Even small interventions can build up to making a change, making it more uncomfortable for men to act in this way, even if it doesn't happen right away. Men speaking to men has the potential to make the biggest impact, particularly because they are more likely to listen to other men than women.

Sometimes a straight call-out of a man behaving badly is what is needed but even this does not have to be a hot-headed confrontation. Try presenting another viewpoint, clearly expressing disagreement or challenging their assumptions by asking them to explain what they mean (even if you know full well what they meant). Use language like 'Do you realise what you just said was really inappropriate?', 'I've heard it explained differently' or 'Comments like that can be damaging because ...' It might feel as though it is just going to make it awkward, but this is a chance to provide information. In those little moments of bravery, where men break away from the pack, one does not need to change everyone's mind right away to feel it was worth doing: we are starting by planting small seeds of dissent. A nudge in a different direction.

This is one of many ways of men disrupting accepted norms in small day-to-day moments rather than a single 'smash glass in case of emergency' toolkit that only allows men to intervene in volatile and high-stakes moments when violence has reached its peak. This book is really about prompting men to see change as much broader than what to do at the moment of conflict, to whack-a-mole the issue back without actually digging out what caused it in the first place. Why does that man feel he is entitled to speak to his girlfriend in that way? This is about seeing how dynamics of gender and power between men and women are causing harm, not just knowing what to do when we see it unravelling in front of us.

Having a discussion with a friend about their behaviour at a later point might seem like the more cowardly option in the moment than publicly calling it out, but it could be more fruitful in the long term than embarrassing him at the table. This is why men developing their own understanding of the problem, and their place in it, is crucial because it allows them to make these decisions rather than waiting for a woman to tell them what to do and when, which isn't going to be a transformative long-term change. Men want to be able to take what they are learning about themselves and the changes needed and share that with others.

Jamie Klingler of Reclaim These Streets told me that in an ideal world we would see these behaviours emerge among men organically. She gave the example of men travelling in a car together: 'You're 17, you're in a car with your three guy friends, and one yells something at a girl [on the street]. You want the other guys to say like: "Yo, that's fucked up. Don't do that to that girl. That's not fucking cool. She's gonna go home and be nervous about that. You scared that woman." That's where we want to get to where men are policing themselves. That's the goal.' For Eliza Hatch of *Cheer Up Luv* this is also about smaller, everyday incidents: 'In a crowded room, if you see a man dominating a conversation and saying something sexist, you could say, "I think differently." You don't have to be as bold as shoving yourself into conflict.' A campaign orchestrated by Andy Burnham, Mayor of Greater Manchester, in 2021, tried to encourage men to do just this. It asked them: 'Is This Ok?' against a montage of everyday sexual harassment. The video was addressed specifically at men – a marked departure from the avalanche of campaigns targeted at women. It was viewed over 5,000,000 times on Twitter and is being taken into schools and colleges in the region in 2022.

Research shows that the bystander approach does work. A survey of soldiers given bystander training showed that, compared to soldiers who did not take part, they were 'significantly more likely' to have helped an acquaintance or a stranger. Studies in schools showed the same thing. Fundamentally, this comes down to men feeling they have a responsibility to speak out, whether that is among friends or in their role as a father, as a colleague, a manager, a teacher, an educator, a faith leader or someone role modelling to young men in a different capacity. Not just waiting for someone else, normally a woman, to do that instead.

For the man who confronted the bouncer, it is understandable that he felt like his efforts had not come to fruition, but that isn't the end of the road. He should take strength from it having led to a conversation with his girlfriend about what she needs from him, having reached out to try and broaden his education on this topic, and he could still speak more with his friends and family about the changes he is trying to make in his own life and why they should do the same. The change doesn't have to happen in one moment, it will be a process.

The bystander approach should not be seen as a solitary takeaway, but as part of the larger programme of work we detailed in the previous chapter. Men should be wary about jumping to educate or give ill-advised lectures to other men before they have their own house in order. This includes identifying themselves as part of the problem, addressing gender and sexual norms that subordinate women, developing understanding of blindspots and confronting deeply held assumptions about women that mean men still do this work in name only. Bringing other men and boys into the learning is a secondary stage that only works if men are willing to address where they have personally gone wrong, too – this is where one has complete control.

In beginning this work there is no time like the present, but for many men it might feel like the first hurdle is not having all the answers – stopped in their tracks by not being able to resolve this problem right away. While we want to avoid doing ineffective or potentially harmful work, men must also know that not having all the answers isn't a roadblock to utility.

13

Don't Have All the Answers

The sun was going down and the temperature was dropping towards freezing. On a street corner in residential north London, hundreds of people stood in silence. Many were holding candles and lighters, the hot wax running down their fingers; others carried bouquets of flowers, tealights and notes scrawled on large scraps of cardboard or tucked into tiny, private folds of paper. The crowd had grown so large, many couldn't see the performance being held on the steps of the London Irish Centre, obscured by hedges and parked cars, and instead were craning their necks to listen to the music. Some were crying. I felt rage.

It was January 2022. Less than a year since thousands of women, and some men, across the UK had done the same for Sarah Everard. And less than three months since the same had taken place for Sabina Nessa. It reached 4 p.m. and as we stood at the vigil, the street lights flickered on around us, signalling the arrival of darkness. At the same time three days earlier primary-school teacher Ashling Murphy was killed while going for a run after work in Tullamore, County Offaly, Ireland. Ashling was 23 years old. As if the frequency of violence against women wasn't painstakingly obvious enough given the regularity of these vigils, the point was laboured even further as she was killed on a canal path named Fiona's Way – in honour of Fiona Pender, a pregnant woman who went missing in 1996 and was never found.

In the wake of Murphy's death, the trauma for many women was compounded as the #NotAllMen narrative emerged at full throttle. Katie Hannon, a presenter on Ireland's national broadcaster, RTÉ, received an anonymous email just before going on air, telling her that if she 'solicited negative comments about men [on her show], you will have to personally answer for it'. Elsewhere, a man used a Zoom vigil, held in Murphy's honour, as a chance to expose himself and masturbate on camera in front of hundreds of attendees. The full spectrum of men's violence spewed to the surface, its toxicity indisputable.

Violence against women is a public emergency, an epidemic, and as such will not have an overnight fix. Although this seems obvious looking at the scale of the problem and how deep its roots run into the bedrock of our society, it can present conflict when asking men to commit to help. One of the roles assigned to men by the Man Box is the role of fixer. This can often compel men to want to only provide solutions, to resolve something. To feel like anything less than being able to say 'job done' equates to an outright failure, a dereliction of duty as a man. While an immediate remedy would be worth its weight in gold, men are not being asked to provide women's salvation. They should not expect to have all the answers here. To come in, take over and resolve the problem single-handedly.

This cold reality should not be a reason for despair but rather seeing individual learning as part of a much bigger movement. This goes way beyond one person and even one lifetime. We are laying the foundations for a better future, just as we have the privilege of standing on the shoulders of those who came before us. To be a valuable contributor, you do not need to mend everything or know it all. Sophie Francis-Cansfield, policy and public affairs manager at Women's Aid, says: 'We're not asking men and boys to jump in and solve everything…and we're not asking them to hand out advice when they're not experts. We're not asking for a lot, it's the listening and believing, and moving from being a bystander to an upstander. You are one part of everything that is needed but at the moment we do not even have that.'

Here, men must be helping to do two pieces of work in tandem – the emergency fire fighting (which should be funded appropriately rather than relentlessly subject to damaging cuts) and the future proofing to get to a place where the fire fighting is no longer required. 'But across society we are phenomenally bad at that,' says Sophie Walker. This is why the work required has to be disruptive, not only to individual men but to the male template that our lives are dictated by in the media, culture and society. It has to be a structural change.

As well as accepting that this will be life-long learning, a process, men should accept that they might not always get things right. While they should endeavour not to cause harm to the women they are supporting, they should also see that mistakes are possible in new territory. Professor Burrell says this means it is crucial men are receptive to feedback. 'No matter how much you read, you are going to make mistakes because this system has had such an impact on us all. The way we think, behave, see the world as normal,' he says. 'Being open to being accountable and seeking out feedback from women – am I doing okay? If someone says maybe you're taking up too much space, do not be defensive, take that on board.'

Using this work as a way to alleviate feelings of guilt or shame over past behaviour is not what women need – nor should the movement be seen as a rotating door for the rehabilitation of men who know their digressions and abuse have harmed women. Affiliating yourself with this movement cannot be a way to masquerade cruelty or malpractice. Accountability in this field is absolutely vital. But neither should men be deterred by the hard work of self-improvement and consciousness-raising. Eliza Hatch, founder of *Cheer Up Luv*, says that this is important looking to the future: 'Men need to be held accountable for their actions. I also think there is room for more nuance and holding out a hand instead of being, like, we're going to build a fucking wall and you're on this side or that,' she says. 'It's like you have to be on one side of the fence or the other and I really don't like that. You can be an ally and a feminist without it having to be a political stamp or a culture war thing.'

In putting your head above the parapet men will likely invite scrutiny of their behaviour from other men and women. This work should never be used as a shield against a personal history of violence or unacceptable behaviour. But it is also possible to use criticism to inform personal change. This is not to say that you can be a domestic abuser one week and an advocate for women the next. But choosing to do this work is not, as sociologist Michael Flood told me, 'a badge of perfection or purity': 'It's not a claim that one has never behaved in poor or sleazy or even coercive ways towards women. But it's a symbol of one's commitment to never do that again, to speak out against that,' he says. 'Men have to take responsibility, we have to make amends, we have to change our behaviour. But men are human like everyone else.'

Professor Nicole Westmarland agrees that in having open conversations about the risks that men present to the movement, we can plan for the risks: 'I think a lot of men are worried and scared about getting caught and being called out about this and we need to stop the stereotype that, like, somebody is a perpetrator or not a perpetrator and accept that most men have used some form of discrimination against women.' Instead of discounting any man who has ever behaved in these inappropriate ways, we can begin to shift to a more productive and accountable form of allyship that is less about men marching in and rescuing women and more about listening to what women need with renewed commitment to the cause.

Men should see all this as a positive challenge rather than fearing all the ways they cannot and will not succeed. Dan Guinness from Beyond Equality says when he first started this work he saw himself as 'more of a saviour' than part of the problem: 'Then I have been confronted by people in my life, who have pointed out the harm that I've done. I've been educated many, many times and challenged, especially by women in my life.' These are learning moments. Instead of seeing challenges as a bucket of cold water thrown on enthusiasm, it is crucial for men to see that, yes, they might be challenged but that they should embrace this and do better.

There are some men who we are never going to reach with this work. Instead, we should look to the majority who are not perpetrating violence, but might have behaved in ways they are not proud of in the past, passively benefitting from sexism and the inequality of women. These men need to be receptive to the message, to believing and hearing women, to being allies when it might not be popular with other men, to being open to learning and to ending ways they have behaved poorly.

Because this change requires shifting our very environment, it might be easier to think about it as a long-term shift, like tectonic plates moving slowly but surely, rather than an abrupt earthquake that pulls the rug from under us. Joni van de Sand, global co-director of the MenEngage Alliance, uses a Dutch phrase: 'We are mopping the floor while the tap is running' (meaning that you are working to fix a problem while it persists).

As with the changes required for combating the climate emergency, we should be heartened not deterred that this work might extend beyond what we are capable of doing as individuals and in our lifetime. Dr Vera-Gray says: 'This is about generational change. We need to think that far ahead so it starts to become possible. This is going to extend beyond our lifetime.'

An educational piece should be taking place in age-appropriate ways throughout schools and higher education. Engaging children from early on before harmful attitudes have a chance to become entrenched. As we've seen, this isn't just about teaching people about violence or sexual relationships, but about concepts like respect for women, listening to their voices, valuing their contributions and having empathy. This can be done with children of all ages, in mixed-sex groups that teach mutual respect and value. Even over something as small as sharing a pencil. Andrea Simon, director of the End Violence Against Women Coalition (EVAW), says: 'It has got to be linked back to healthy, respectful relationships education.' Doing such work should be a policy priority for governments and leaders, understood for the phenomenal transformative potential it could have. This also applies to helping parents and family speak to their sons and young boys about these issues in appropriate ways.

For adults, we should see campaigns set up in the same way we use public health messaging to change behaviours around smoking, seatbelt wearing, or drink-driving, shifting attitudes around acceptability of these behaviours meaning people start to see it as something they do not want to do, something that is harmful and has consequences. These should be planned as multi-year campaigns, decades even, that reinforce the messages across a period of time rather than a short blip that dies down quickly. We know that a rollout of such society-wide messaging is possible, as we have seen in the recent example of the Covid-19 pandemic. When there is political appetite and public will, messaging can be impactful and effective. And there is evidence that the public is open to seeing change. A VAWG government consultation that was reopened for submissions after the murder of Sarah Everard received 160,000 responses in two weeks and a total of 180,000 responses across the whole period it was open – unheard of in this type of research. When asked what should be the government's priority, the most popular answer was 'more action to prevent violence against women and girls from happening – for example, education programmes in schools to teach children about these crimes'.

But we cannot wait for governments or administrations to lead the charge, for the right political moment, the next election window or another paper that the UK government wants to make its toothless legacy. We must start to make change and we don't need all the men in the world, or even in our town, to be on side to start to do this: we can create a broad movement with whoever is willing to put in the time and energy. 'You don't need a mass movement of men,' pioneering activist Jackson Katz tells me. 'You just need a critical mass.' It will require money and political will, which men and women can achieve through canvassing and pressure.

We can begin to move the dial bit by bit.

Men do not need all the answers to step forward and be counted. They do not need a 10-step plan for how to fix this problem to be of use. Men who are committed to changing their own behaviour, to calling out those around them, to doing the work, to listening and learning and striving for change are those we need on the frontlines. This will not be an easy quest – in fact, for men who have enjoyed male privilege, sometimes equality can feel as if it is relative discrimination – and at points you are likely to get dragged back into the old ways of operating. Progress is rarely linear, but by picking up this book you've started the ball rolling, as has every other man who knows, deep down, he wants a different world for women and for himself.

It is long overdue.

Conclusion

I started writing this book because I was angry. Furious, in fact. I was incensed that it has so long been accepted that women are both the cause of the violence they face – for what they wear, for where they walk, for what they drink, for being too friendly, for not being friendly enough – and burdened with coming up with the solution too. It is a double-bind that is inescapable, insufferable and exhausting, as it has been for generations of women and girls. Compounded for many by additional weights of racism, ableism or homophobia.

But I was also angry about the smaller aggressions that women face every day, most of which presumably go unnoticed by men, but never fail to remind women of our inequality and perceived lesser value. My male partner always being handed the card machine when paying the bill at a restaurant because there is a presumption the money must be his rather than mine; the washing machine repair man only talking to my male partner in the house even though I was the one who organised the visit; my female friends being called first when their child needs picking up from nursery even though they are not listed as the primary contact, because their work is seen as more interruptible; the lack of baby changing tables in men's toilets because women must always be doing this messy work.

These things might seem utterly insignificant, but they speak to the fact women spend a lifetime tiptoeing around the centrality and superiority of men as dictated and sustained by our history, our legislation, our culture, our media, the sex we have, the porn we watch, the language we use and much more. Moulding our brains, our words and bodies into the spaces men deem suitable – mother, caregiver, sex object, wife, slut. Our culture of impeccably low standards tells us to shrug off sexism, to tolerate it. But at the sharp end of all these inequalities is outright violence – the murder, the rape, the assault, the violation of women. The root cause of which is the systematic devaluation and degradation of women in every field. Although the reasons men commit violence are not one-dimensional, it only exists at such a scale because the conditions are ripe: the environment is just the right temperature for its cultivation.

For too long the elephant in the room has been that gender-based violence is portrayed as untethered from everything else around it. Floating around as an abstract concept, something done by freakish monsters who pervert the natural order in acting out rather than embodying it. Something that is unpredictable and can only be stopped by women being more vigilant. But not any more, for women can see the transparency in this reverse logic. As Martin Luther King wrote, 'there comes a time when the cup of endurance runs over'.

We should feel ashamed at being content asking women to rely on smart straws that go blue if rohypnol, GHB or ketamine is added to their drink while they dance with friends. In telling them to use a hair scrunchie that transforms into a drink cover so their glass is sealed at all times. Trying to sell them anti-rape underwear that is essentially a chastity belt but might buy them a few more seconds before a rapist has them undressed. Encouraging them to use a specially designed hotline when walking home so a trained dispatcher can coach them and keep them calm, asking: 'How far away are you?' Or in promising to install more street lights and CCTV to capture their assault in high definition. We still hear police officers telling women to carry drug testing kits on nights out, 'very much like having condoms' they reassure, and repeated requests for harsher policing, beefed-up security and legally mandated bag checks at nightclubs (note that any lean towards reliance on police, law-enforcement or carceral solutions disproportionately impact marginalised people). Some of these ideas are well-intentioned, many designed by women, but none of it stops the misogyny – none of it changes the fact that some men feel entitled to use and abuse women.

Yes, we must use some crutches to help us navigate a dangerous world for women while we work towards a better future. But in looking to technology or innovations for answers we often feel the job is done and dusted, giving ourselves a pat on the back, confusing temporary platitudes for long-term cures. Why are we still so afraid of talking about prevention at the root? We can see how little has changed when we look at a segment written in the WLM *Red Rag* magazine 50 years ago that could have been written today: 'We constantly come back to the point that after years of "politicising" men, the kind of problems which arise in personal relations go on the same roundabouts, the same pathways and the same compromises, year after year,' later adding, 'we do as women have always done – stare at the ceiling and wonder if we are quietly going mad; that only we seem to believe that a problem actually exists.' We can no longer comfort ourselves with mealy-mouthed excuses or half-baked, knee-jerk strategies where we outsource the solution to women. After the death of Ashling Murphy, Sarah Benson, CEO of Women's Aid Ireland, articulated this point (and pain) perfectly: 'We must not fall into tired tropes of examining whether areas are "safe" but consider instead the attitudes and actions of men who make women feel unsafe even in crowded and well lit areas. Women are not afraid of the dark or a lonely space. They are afraid of a violent male perpetrator in the dark.'

Real change will come when we start to address the over-whelming perpetrators of violence against women – men. This is about changing the problem from the ground up: where it starts, not where it ends. We are looking to change behaviours and poisonous attitudes that can prevent violence from happening, not just implementing better ways to deal with the aftershocks. We must collectively accept the whole barrel we operate in is rotten, not just a couple of apples. The most effective way of keeping women safe is interrupting the harms before they happen. This will require changing our understanding of who is responsible for these solutions from only women to everyone.

As well as more pragmatic changes – more funding, better integration of VAWG experts across all parts of government, factoring gender harm into all policies, adapting educational materials to ensure boys are learning about this in an age-appropriate manner as early as possible, amplifying a range of women's voices, transformation of the criminal justice system and much more – it is also about future-proofing changes by ensuring they challenge cyber violence as well as in person. Any policy that treats harms in the online world as lesser or separate does not have an understanding of how the digital and real world are symbiotic.

We are beginning to see campaigns that are unafraid to shout about this. Police Scotland's *That Guy* campaign, launched in September 2021, chose to go against the grain and focused on a bystander-style approach, telling men as potential perpetrators to change their behaviour, rather than victims. DCC Malcolm Graham, deputy chief constable for crime and operations at Police Scotland, told me on a call: 'The message [needed to] embrace the majority as being responsible for creating an environment in which these acts were neither permitted nor enabled and encouraged.' DCC Graham saw it as the natural next step for his force to focus its attention 'on where we felt that [the] problem, and therefore the solutions lay'. It was not the first time Police Scotland had focused on men in their communications but it has gained more traction this time. Hackney Council in London also put up billboards with the slogan: 'You are in Hackney. Here men and boys should help keep women and girls safe'.

In March 2022, shortly before the first anniversary of Sarah Everard's kidnapping, the Home Office released its own campaign, Enough Is Enough, which also encouraged people to call out harassment and violence against women. Unlike the other campaigns, it asks both men and women to be bystanders. The Mayor of London, Sadiq Khan, has also released a campaign saying that the problem is not just violent men but men who engage in sexist behaviour and stand by silently while others harass or hurt. Mr Khan said: 'If we are going to truly fix the problem of violence against women and girls we need to see a fundamental cultural shift which puts the onus of responsibility on men.' Camilla, Duchess of Cornwall, has also appeared on national radio, saying things like 'rapists are not born, they are constructed' and 'we do need a whole culture change'. There is some solace to be found that this level of nuanced understanding is now being reached by our leaders.

These campaigns that work to address the causes of the problem, rather than extinguishing the fires they cause, do offer a glimmer of hope that the tide might be beginning to turn. Even if they sometimes feel more a gesture of goodwill, of political placation, than a catalyst for radical change that will shake the patriarchal table, they do suggest that it won't always be the case that women will be blamed for the violence put upon them, that there could be another way. A major survey of women's groups, conducted in early 2022 by charity Rosa, found 89 per cent of people thought there had been a shift in public awareness of the issue in the preceding 12 months. Perhaps the scales have finally fallen from people's eyes.

Although I am angry and upset at the repeated pain inflicted upon women at the hands of men, I also believe strongly in the capacity for hope. Feminism by its very nature believes that things can get better, that we are not beyond change. That the status quo is not concrete and walls that seem permanent can be moved. Belief that the struggle is worth the endurance and persistence it requires. That sexist practices can become the old ways, not the always. Because while people are the very thing that maintains unequal systems, they are also what can topple a system too. I believe that the future will see gender equality. It might not be in my lifetime or yours, but it will come.

Early on, we discussed the fallacy of suggesting this work was anti-men. I see those who cling tightly to 'boys will be boys' as setting the bar lowest for men, relegating them to poor behaviour as par for the course. We all know that most men are so much better and stronger than this, capable of inciting and provoking change. And when we create safety for women, we also unlock space for men to be the best versions of themselves. In the 1999 film *The Matrix*, the protagonist is given a choice between taking a red pill (that will show him the world as it really is) or a blue pill (that lets him continue in blissful ignorance). Doing this work is a version of that, of seeing that we are living in a default man world. Although a world tailored to men might have long been comfortable for them, it brings with it so much pain.

Until this point you may never have needed to confront this beast head-on. Consider this your wake-up call, your moment to do so. I believe there are many men out there who want to do more. Men who broadly support movements like #MeToo but are unsure about specifically what to do, immobilised by concern about doing 'the right thing' rather than doing anything. This becomes paralysing and, crucially, unhelpful. Reading *How Men Can Help*, men must feel the urgency that women have always felt. This is your shared struggle now too.

Giving all women the right to walk home alone at night, without fear of being attacked, is both the simplest demand and seemingly still the most radical. Because it shows just how far we have to go, even with all the talk of progress. Men now must ask – as women have long done – how do we change the world so that women can be free?

Acknowledgements

The first thank you has to go to my publisher, Oliver Holden-Rea, who approached me with this idea for a book shortly after I had quit my job and was wondering where my life was going next. I am grateful that Oli trusted me with his vision, united as we are in our strong belief that it is time to put men's violence in the spotlight. Thank you to Oli for thoughtful edits that have always made the book stronger; for leaving me to recover from Covid as much as was possible on a very tight deadline; and for saying you felt nervous in our Zoom edit meeting. It reassured me. I hope I have done justice to the book you wanted to see in the world.

Also to Oli for allowing me to find my wonderful literary agent Angelique Tran Van Sang, who helped me navigate the waters of publishing as a total novice, giving me the knowledge and support that I didn't even know I would need. Angelique answered all of my stupid questions, was always available at the end of the phone, and never seemed phased that I kept emailing at fairly annoying times. Thank you for your patience, good humour and kindness. And thanks for making me part of the Felicity Bryan family.

Thank you to all of the wider team at Welbeck Publishing Group who have worked at different stages on *How Men Can Help*, for your creativity, ideas and hard work. I am very grateful to have a team behind the idea as writing can often feel like a lonely endeavour. Special thanks to Jane Donovan for your rapid copyediting, even with laptop troubles.

All of the experts who fit me into their busy schedules – especially as most of these meetings were at short notice, across multiple time zones, just before Christmas – thank you. As a journalist I am always so pleasantly surprised by how generous people are with their time and their knowledge, without compensation, but I was especially touched this time around.

Thank you to Jackson Katz, Michael Flood, Clare McGlynn, Fiona Vera-Gray, Stephen Burrell, Sandy Ruxton, Rachel Thompson, Dan Guinness, Mike Taggart, Nicole Westmarland, Malcolm Graham, Loretta Trickett, Janey Starling, Seyi Falodun-Liburd, Ryan Hart, Jasmine Mohammad, Jamie Klingler, Sophie Walker, Sue Fish, Andrea Simon, Mark Hegarty, Imogen Greenwood, Kezia Mbonye, Eliza Hatch, Maya Tutton, Women's Aid, the MenEngage Alliance, NOMAS, and many others, for your time and conversations with me that were often longer than I'd promised. And to Len Pennie for allowing me to use your beautiful words, and for sharing your poems with us in the first place.

I am also indebted to all of the women (and the few men) who have shared their experiences with me over the years I have written about the topic of gender violence. From the early days of cyber flashing reporting, through to pandemic Zoom interviews, I am always stunned by your openness and feel honoured to be allowed to tell your stories to the world.

To Harriet Hall for being a wonderful editor and friend, for reading over a very early draft and sending encouraging notes on WhatsApp when you had many other more important things to be doing instead. To the strong women who have mentored and edited me throughout my career, giving me opportunities, words of advice, and frankly a big push when required: Poorna Bell, Amy Packham, Vicky Frost, Polly Curtis, Jess Brammar, Eleanor Jones.

My dear friends who show me every day what it means to be a loyal and brilliant woman. Listing all the names feels like a fool's errand, but I have to mention Holly, Harris, Lauren, Lucy, Joanne, and Izzy. To the rest of you, thank you for the love (and the commissions) you've given me, and for being the most enthusiastic cheerleaders. I still can't believe how quickly you all pre-ordered. Especially to you Karina, how could I forget my Caribbean fanbase who knew me before anyone paid me to write? And to the many other people in the industry who have supported me from the sidelines, in the private messages and tweets, when they had nothing to gain, and no reason other than kindness.

To my family, spread over oceans but always in my heart. How lucky I am to be surrounded by such unwavering love, strength and support. To Sazzy, to Mum, to Dad. Thank you for allowing me the space and time to work out that writing was my calling and always being ready to dispense advice or let me take over your living room floor for a month to write my book. And to my T, you keep me alive (literally feeding me and forcing me to eat salad) and never complain about yet another walk where I moan about work. You are my constant and a testament to the brilliance of men. I could not feel luckier.

Lastly, it would be remiss to not thank the Pomodoro Technique, which kept me on the straight and narrow (in 25-minute chunks) when Twitter or another chocolate biscuit seemed a much more tempting prospect than starting a new chapter. Committing 50,000 words to paper in under 4 weeks was no joke, so it was good to have a helping hand.

Useful Resources

Support Organisations

Women's Aid, https://www.womensaid.org.uk/
End Violence Against Women, https://www.endviolenceagainst
women.org.uk/
Refuge, https://www.refuge.org.uk/
Imkaan, https://www.imkaan.org.uk/
White Ribbon, https://www.whiteribbon.org.uk/
Beyond Equality, https://www.beyondequality.org/
MenEngage, https://menengage.org/

Introduction

Fiona Vera-Gray, *The Right Amount of Panic: How Women Trade
Freedom For Safety*
https://www.theguardian.com/uk-news/2021/oct/23/hundreds-of-
uk-drink-spiking-reports-in-the-past-two-months
https://www.everyonesinvited.uk/
https://www.bbc.co.uk/news/uk-56491643
https://www.telegraph.co.uk/news/2021/10/01/call-999-have-doubts-
police-officer-says-minister/

https://www.independent.co.uk/news/uk/home-news/met-police-sarah-everard-advice-criticism-b1930682.html

https://www.bbc.co.uk/news/uk-england-york-north-yorkshire-58915325

https://www.independent.co.uk/news/uk/home-news/women-earphones-night-london-tube-police-warning-victim-blaming-a8577656.html

https://www.skynews.com.au/australia-news/uk-women-slam-guest-on-morning-show-who-advised-women-to-wear-running-shoes-to-avoid-late-night-attacks/video/ad4cb24885483ea76e10ceaa1
3313492

https://www.bbc.co.uk/news/uk-england-london-58661926

https://www.met.police.uk/cp/crime-prevention/protect-yourself-from-crime/stay-safe/

https://www.theguardian.com/lifeandstyle/2021/oct/09/bt-888-phone-service-women-walking-home

https://www.youtube.com/watch?v=McDTvubLhgc

https://blogs.lse.ac.uk/businessreview/2019/08/24/gender-equality-improves-life-satisfaction-for-men-and-women/

https://www.theguardian.com/books/2021/jul/09/why-do-so-few-men-read-books-by-women

https://www.globalcitizen.org/en/content/half-of-young-men-oppose-feminism-uk/

https://www.ons.gov.uk/peoplepopulationandcommunity/crimeandjustice/articles/
thelastingimpactofviolenceagainstwomenandgirls/2021-11-24

Accept Violence Against Women Happens - Even If You Don't See It

Cheer Up Luv, https://www.cheerupluv.com/

https://www.tandfonline.com/doi/full/10.1080/01924036.2020.173 2435

https://www.femicidecensus.org/wp-content/uploads/2020/11/ Femicide-Census-10-year-report.pdf

https://www.bbc.co.uk/news/explainers-56365412

https://www.eurekalert.org/news-releases/494477

https://rapecrisis.org.uk/get-informed/about-sexual-violence/ statistics-sexual-violence/

https://www.ons.gov.uk/peoplepopulationandcommunity/crimeand justice/datasets/natureofsexualassaultbyrapeorpenetration englandandwales

https://www.ons.gov.uk/peoplepopulationandcommunity/crime andjustice/bulletins/domesticabuseinenglandandwalesoverview/ november2020

https://www.sisofrida.org/wp-content/uploads/2020/05/The-impact-of-COVID-19-on-Disabled-women-from-Sisters-of-Frida.pdf

https://www.womensaid.org.uk/information-support/what-is-domestic-abuse/domestic-abuse-is-a-gendered-crime/

https://www.theguardian.com/uk-news/2021/jul/07/women-girls-facing-epidemic-violence-police-watchdog-warns-england-wales

https://www.ons.gov.uk/peoplepopulationandcommunity/crime andjustice/articles/natureofsexualassaultbyrapeorpenetration englandandwales/yearendingmarch2020#reporting-sexual-assault-to-the-police

https://829ef90d-0745-49b2-b404-cbea85f15fda.filesusr.com/ugd/ f98049_a0f11db6395a48fbbac0e40da899dcb8.pdf

https://www.refuge.org.uk/refuge-better-protection-of-black-women-domestic-abuse/

http://usir.salford.ac.uk/id/eprint/46973/3/Journal%20of%20Interpersonal%20Violence,%20Connelly,%20Kamerade,%20Sanders%20(accepted).pdf:public

https://www.crimeandjustice.org.uk/sites/crimeandjustice.org.uk/files/09627250008552877.pdf

https://www.theguardian.com/society/2020/jul/14/we-are-facing-the-decriminalisation-of-warns-victims-commissioner

https://www.unwomenuk.org/safe-spaces-now

https://plan-uk.org/file/what-works-for-ending-sexual-harassment-report-executive-summary/download?token=NojlmO9m

http://activityinequality.stanford.edu/

https://www.tuc.org.uk/news/nearly-two-three-young-women-have-experienced-sexual-harassment-work-tuc-survey-reveals

https://www.girlguiding.org.uk/globalassets/docs-and-resources/research-and-campaigns/girls-attitudes-survey-2015.pdf

https://www.theguardian.com/education/2021/jun/10/sexual-harassment-is-a-routine-part-of-life-schoolchildren-tell-ofsted

https://www.independent.co.uk/life-style/women/office-national-statistics-women-safety-b1907807.html

https://plan-uk.org/media-centre/1-in-5-girls-have-experienced-street-harassment-during-lockdown

https://www.amnesty.org.uk/online-abuse-women-widespread

https://www.amnesty.org.uk/online-violence-women-mps

https://www.theguardian.com/politics/2017/sep/05/diane-abbott-more-abused-than-any-other-mps-during-election

https://time.com/3082038/roxane-gay-interview-bad-feminist/

https://www.theguardian.com/politics/video/2021/oct/06/dominic-raab-confuses-meaning-of-misogyny-and-rejects-it-as-a-hate-video

https://hansard.parliament.uk/Commons/2021-03-11/debates/
D1B46B57-F176-4EB4-9729-66D164FBBB7E/International
Women%E2%80%99SDay

https://www.youtube.com/watch?v=b1XGPvbWn0A

Understand It is a Spectrum

Jackson Katz, *The Macho Paradox*

https://www.nytimes.com/2017/10/30/health/men-rape-sexual-
assault.html

https://www.ojp.gov/ncjrs/virtual-library/abstracts/characteristics-
undetected-rapists-perspectives-victimology-1979

https://www.ted.com/talks/jackson_katz_violence_against_
women_it_s_a_men_s_issue

https://twitter.com/KarenAdamMSP/status/1476539866016100352

https://www.thetimes.co.uk/article/somewhere-out-there-drill-
sergeant-exercise-dreams-5knqmft7j

https://www.abc.net.au/news/2014-04-18/meagher-the-danger-
of-the-monster-myth/5399108

https://www.ons.gov.uk/peoplepopulationandcommunity/crime
andjustice/datasets/natureofsexualassaultbyrapeorpenetration
englandandwales

https://www.theguardian.com/australia-news/2019/oct/10/
essential-poll-young-men-least-likely-to-identify-abusive-
domestic-behaviour

https://www.bloomberg.com/graphics/2020-mass-shootings-domestic-
violence-connection/

https://www.theguardian.com/uk-news/2021/sep/30/sarah-everards-
killer-might-have-been-identified-as-threat-sooner-police-admit

https://www.standard.co.uk/news/uk/cps-shops-crown-prosecution-
service-london-b969774.html

https://www.dailymail.co.uk/news/article-9773105/Wayne-Couzens-Devoted-father-hid-dark-desire-rape-kill.html

https://www.thesun.co.uk/news/16764413/monster-dad-raped-abused-daughter-family/

https://babe.net/2018/01/13/aziz-ansari-28355

https://www.vox.com/identities/2019/7/12/20690303/aziz-ansari-sexual-misconduct-accusation-right-now

https://people.com/tv/aziz-ansari-statement-report-sexual-encounter/

https://www.youtube.com/watch?v=gyPoqFcvt9w

https://www.huffingtonpost.co.uk/entry/cyberflashing-why-are-men-still-sending-women-unsolicited-dick-pics_uk_5bdc278fe4b04367a87b755e?utm_hp_ref=uk-cyberflashing

https://link.springer.com/article/10.1023/A:1018868913615

https://journals.sagepub.com/doi/abs/10.1177/0886260519888518

Forget #NotAllMen

bell hooks, *Feminist Theory from Margin to Centre*

Amia Srinivasan, *The Right To Sex*

KEGS Survivors, https://kegssurvivors.com/blog/

http://listen-tome.com/save-me/

https://yougov.co.uk/topics/relationships/articles-reports/2019/03/06/did-gillettes-advert-backfire-because-most-britons

https://twitter.com/jameelajamil/status/1369812466205483008

https://funceji.files.wordpress.com/2017/08/bell_hooks_feminist_theory_from_margin_to_centebookzz-org_.pdf

https://psychology.umbc.edu/files/2016/10/White-Privilege_McIntosh-1989.pdf

https://www.buzzfeednews.com/article/krystieyandoli/terry-crews-said-men-need-to-hold-other-men-accountable-for

Get to Grips With History

Caroline Criado Perez, *Invisible Women*

https://www.newscientist.com/article/mg23831740-400-the-origins-of-sexism-how-men-came-to-rule-12000-years-ago/

https://www.theguardian.com/lifeandstyle/2020/jan/21/what-happens-when-we-dont-believe-women

https://www.theguardian.com/theguardian/from-the-archive-blog/2012/nov/15/el-vino-women-ban-fleet-street-1982

https://inews.co.uk/opinion/married-women-take-husband-name-patriarchy-497605

https://www.vox.com/2015/5/26/8661537/sally-ride-tampons

https://commonslibrary.parliament.uk/research-briefings/sn01250/

http://news.bbc.co.uk/1/hi/uk_politics/4698222.stm

https://www.theguardian.com/commentisfree/2017/jan/24/photo-trump-womens-rights-protest-reproductive-abortion-developing-contries

https://www.theguardian.com/business/2021/oct/07/only-eight-of-uks-top-100-companies-headed-by-women-report-says

https://www.theguardian.com/artanddesign/2021/may/19/why-are-our-cities-built-for-6ft-tall-men-the-female-architects-who-fought-back

https://www.thetimes.co.uk/article/office-temperature-air-con-men-women-sexist-zwvkxpnsd

https://www.theguardian.com/society/2022/jan/04/women-more-likely-die-operation-male-surgeon-study

https://www.bhf.org.uk/what-we-do/news-from-the-bhf/news-archive/2016/august/women-are-50-per-cent-more-likely-than-men-to-be-given-incorrect-diagnosis-following-a-heart-attack

https://www.dbei.med.upenn.edu/research/studies/men-are-more-likely-women-receive-cpr-public-study-finds

https://en.unesco.org/Id-blush-if-I-could

https://data.unwomen.org/publications/whose-time-care-unpaid-care-and-domestic-work-during-covid-19

https://www.bbc.co.uk/news/world-55016842

https://www.theguardian.com/world/2020/may/27/working-mothers-interrupted-more-often-than-fathers-in-lockdown-study

https://www.gov.uk/government/news/employers-do-not-have-to-report-gender-pay-gaps

https://www.theguardian.com/lifeandstyle/2021/oct/11/one-in-six-most-critically-ill-patients-are-unvaccinated-pregnant-women-with-covid

https://www.theguardian.com/commentisfree/2021/oct/29/pregnant-women-vaccinated-covid-mother-child

https://www.theguardian.com/world/2014/apr/15/un-special-rapporteur-manjoo-yarls-wood-home-office

https://www.ethnicity-facts-figures.service.gov.uk/uk-population-by-ethnicity/demographics/male-and-female-populations/1.3

Learn About The Gap

Otegha Uwagba, *We Need To Talk About Money*

Silvia Federici, *Wages Against Housework*

https://www.theguardian.com/world/2018/feb/19/uk-bosses-believe-women-should-say-at-interview-if-they-are-pregnant-report

https://www.acas.org.uk/equal-pay

https://www.ons.gov.uk/employmentandlabourmarket/peopleinwork/earningsandworkinghours/bulletins/genderpaygapintheuk/2021

https://www.fawcettsociety.org.uk/news/the-fawcett-society-announces-date-of-equal-pay-day-2021

https://hbr.org/2018/06/research-women-ask-for-raises-as-often-as-men-but-are-less-likely-to-get-them

https://www.standard.co.uk/news/london/equal-pay-day-2021-uk-
    end-salary-history-campaign-fawcett-society-b966982.html

https://www.theguardian.com/world/2021/dec/06/uk-gender-pay-
    gap-unaffected-by-government-policy-over-past-25-years

https://www.theguardian.com/world/2021/dec/29/gender-pay-
    gap-at-uks-biggest-firms-is-growing-data-suggests

https://www.bbc.co.uk/news/education-51676530

https://www.bbc.co.uk/news/education-39566746

https://www.theguardian.com/lifeandstyle/2009/jul/10/mothers-
    wages-fawcett-society

https://www.thetimes.co.uk/article/motherhood-penalty-cuts-
    earnings-by-up-to-45-zqnlxg3jj

https://assets.publishing.service.gov.uk/government/uploads/system/
    uploads/attachment_data/file/509500/BIS-16-145-pregnancy-
    and-maternity-related-discrimination-and-disadvantage-summary.
    pdf

https://www.theguardian.com/money/2021/oct/15/right-to-
    request-flexible-work-uk-working-mothers

https://www.birmingham.ac.uk/Documents/college-social-sciences/
    business/research/wirc/spl-policy-brief.pdf

https://www.independent.co.uk/life-style/women-men-household-
    chores-domestic-house-gender-norms-a9021586.html?r=43122

https://www.carersuk.org/news-and-campaigns/features/10-facts-
    about-women-and-caring-in-the-uk-on-international-womens-
    day

https://warwick.ac.uk/fac/arts/english/currentstudents/postgraduate/
    masters/modules/femlit/04-federici.pdf

https://www.bl.uk/sisterhood/articles/womens-liberation-a-national-
    movement

https://stats.oecd.org/Index.aspx?DataSetCode=NCC

https://www.theguardian.com/world/2017/may/26/gender-wars-household-chores-comic

https://www.harpersbazaar.com/culture/features/a27259689/toxic-masculinity-male-friendships-emotional-labor-men-rely-on-women/

https://blogs.lse.ac.uk/politicsandpolicy/gendered-impacts-of-austerity-cuts/

https://committees.parliament.uk/publications/4597/documents/46478/default/

https://www.gov.uk/government/news/tampon-tax-abolished-from-today

https://www.endviolenceagainstwomen.org.uk/wp-content/uploads/Joint-Briefing-for-Meg-Hillier-MP-Debate-EVAW-Imkaan.pdf

https://www.weforum.org/reports/global-gender-gap-report-2021/digest

Examine Your Masculinity

Liz Plank, *For The Love Of Men*

https://www.theguardian.com/lifeandstyle/womens-blog/2016/jul/26/womans-murder-called-understandable-lance-hart

https://www.itv.com/news/calendar/2016-07-19/three-dead-identified-as-builders-merchant-wife-and-daughter

https://committees.parliament.uk/work/1605/preventing-violence-against-women-and-girls/

https://assets.publishing.service.gov.uk/government/uploads/system/uploads/attachment_data/file/952527/Changing_Gender_Norms-_Engaging_with_Men_and_Boys.pdf

https://www.who.int/violence_injury_prevention/violence/gender.pdf

https://www.smh.com.au/lifestyle/the-way-we-talk-to-girls-is-different-from-the-way-we-talk-to-boys-20170123-gtwwm4.html

https://www.ted.com/talks/tony_porter_a_call_to_men/transcript?
language=en#t-326468

https://www.gq.com/story/liz-plank-mindful-masculinity-and-
marie-kondo-approach

https://commonslibrary.parliament.uk/research-briefings/cbp-7749/

https://www.mentalhealth.org.uk/a-to-z/m/men-and-mental-health

https://www.theguardian.com/society/2016/nov/05/men-less-likely-
to-get-help--mental-health

https://journals.sagepub.com/doi/abs/10.1177/1359105314551623

https://www.bbc.co.uk/news/world-53446827

https://inews.co.uk/news/politics/covid-vaccine-gender-gap-uk-young-
women-more-likely-get-jab-men-1174975

https://www.sciencedirect.com/science/article/abs/pii/S0277953
699003901

https://www.independent.co.uk/climate-change/sustainable-living/
climate-crisis-toxic-masculinity-environment-b1956739.html

https://www.ons.gov.uk/peoplepopulationandcommunity/crime
andjustice/articles/drugmisuseinenglandandwales/yearending
march2020

https://www.huffingtonpost.co.uk/entry/men-friendship-crisis_l_5dbc
9aa7e4b0576b62a1e90f

https://www.bbc.com/worklife/article/20210712-paternity-leave-the-
hidden-barriers-keeping-men-at-work

https://www.researchgate.net/publication/342095143_Swallowing_
the_Black_Pill_A_Qualitative_Exploration_of_Incel_
Antifeminism_within_Digital_Society

https://www.newscientist.com/article/mg23831740-900-why-the-
patriarchy-isnt-good-for-men-and-how-to-fix-it/#ixzz7Hf
W6Ufma

https://www.theguardian.com/commentisfree/2019/jan/15/
    gillette-ad-not-pc-guff-piers-morgan-macho-stereotype-boys

Ask If You're Being Sold To

http://news.bbc.co.uk/1/hi/entertainment/tv_and_radio/2162307.stm
http://news.bbc.co.uk/1/hi/wales/1737528.stm
https://www.theguardian.com/media/interactive/2011/nov/28/
    charlotte-church-witness-statement-leveson-inquiry
https://www.theguardian.com/media/2006/jun/13/bbc.radio
https://www.youtube.com/watch?v=Uy8yLaoWybk
https://www.endviolenceagainstwomen.org.uk/campaign/media-s
    exism-pornography/
https://www.telegraph.co.uk/women/sex/10508530/Boobs-on-Page-
    3-Why-does-a-Tory-MP-think-that-getting-your-tits-out-is-a-
    national-institution.html
https://www.independent.co.uk/voices/comment/no-more-page-3-
    our-grassroots-campaign-took-on-a-huge-corporation-and-we-
    won-9992371.html
https://www.theguardian.com/media/2015/jan/22/the-sun-
    topless-women-page-3
https://www.bbc.co.uk/news/world-43197774
https://www.bbc.co.uk/news/newsbeat-50052155
https://inews.co.uk/sport/olympics/olympics-kit-rules-explained-
    beach-volleyball-bikinis-size-tokyo-2020-restrictions-1114025
https://www.independent.co.uk/life-style/women/germany-
    gymnastics-women-olympics-unitard-b1889197.html
https://www.bbc.co.uk/news/uk-england-nottinghamshire-49035175
https://www.bbc.co.uk/news/business-36595898
https://www.lettoysbetoys.org.uk/the-2021-let-toys-be-toys-
    silliness-awards/

https://www.nbcnews.com/id/wbna30709961

https://www.huffingtonpost.co.uk/entry/bic-pen-for-her-
amazon-reviews_n_1842991

https://www.bbc.co.uk/news/uk-42944833

https://www.theguardian.com/uk-news/2018/oct/18/kleenex-drops-
mansize-branding-from-tissue-boxes-after-complaints-sexism

https://www.bbc.co.uk/news/business-40916607

https://www.youtube.com/watch?v=koPmuEyP3a0

https://twitter.com/piersmorgan/status/1084891133757587456

https://www.independent.co.uk/arts-entertainment/tv/features/
doctor-who-politically-correct-backlash-bbc-jodie-whittaker-
mandip-gill-tosin-cole-a8669156.html

https://www.theguardian.com/fashion/2018/oct/05/topshop-axes-
penguin-pop-up-to-promote-feminist-book-in-store

https://www.bbc.co.uk/news/business-50649826

https://www.theguardian.com/uk-news/2021/jan/28/no-10-pulls-
sexist-covid-ad-showing-all-chores-done-by-women

https://www.theguardian.com/world/2020/jan/21/kfc-apologises-for-
sexist-ad-that-shows-young-boys-staring-at-womans-breasts

Look Beyond Consent

Rachel Thompson, *Rough*

Sophia Smith Galer, *Losing It*

https://metro.co.uk/2015/03/18/dolce-gabbana-in-hot-water-again-
after-gang-rape-ad-campaign-resurfaces-just-days-after-ivf-
furore-5108624/

http://america.aljazeera.com/articles/2015/4/29/bud-light-apology-
highlights-sexism-in-beer-ads.html

https://theweek.com/articles/749978/female-price-male-pleasure

https://www.thecut.com/2020/07/hbo-i-may-destroy-you-review.html

https://www.theguardian.com/lifeandstyle/2017/jan/30/why-is-sex-painful-for-some-women-and-what-can-they-do

https://pubmed.ncbi.nlm.nih.gov/25648245/

https://link.springer.com/article/10.1007/s10508-017-0939-z

https://kinseyinstitute.org/research/faq.php

https://www.theguardian.com/education/2021/jun/10/sexual-harassment-is-a-routine-part-of-life-schoolchildren-tell-ofsted

https://yougov.co.uk/topics/resources/articles-reports/2018/12/01/publics-attitudes-sexual-consent

https://journals.sagepub.com/doi/abs/10.1177/0886260510363421

https://foundationsofgenderstudies.files.wordpress.com/2013/01/catharine-mackinnon-only-words.pdf

https://www.techradar.com/uk/news/porn-sites-attract-more-visitors-than-netflix-and-amazon-youll-never-guess-how-many

https://www.bbc.co.uk/bbcthree/article/bb79a2ce-0de4-4965-98f0-9ebbcfcc2a60

https://www.leverhulme.ac.uk/news/durham-researchers-found-sexually-violent-porn-promoted-first-time-users-top-sites

https://www.stylist.co.uk/news/politics/image-based-sexual-abuse-law/595661

https://www.bbc.co.uk/news/uk-50546184

https://www.childrenscommissioner.gov.uk/wp-content/uploads/2017/06/MDX-NSPCC-OCC-Online-Pornography-Report.pdf

https://www.mic.com/articles/109284/rashida-jones-just-said-the-one-sentence-anyone-who-watches-porn-needs-to-hear

https://www.cypnow.co.uk/news/article/no-relationships-and-sex-education-training-in-four-out-of-five-schools-minister-admits

Challenge Your Assumptions

https://www.independent.co.uk/arts-entertainment/films/features/
harvey-weinstein-rape-trial-victims-court-sentence-prison-metoo-
sex-abuse-a9360131.html

https://www.bbc.co.uk/news/entertainment-arts-40635526

https://www.mcgill.ca/oss/article/history-quackery/history-hysteria

https://www.theguardian.com/politics/2011/apr/27/cameron-sexism-
calm-down-dear

https://www.sciencedaily.com/releases/2021/04/210406164124.htm

https://www.theguardian.com/society/2021/nov/11/black-women-
uk-maternal-mortality-rates

https://www.theatlantic.com/health/archive/2016/03/my-pain-
in-and-of-itself-had-never-been-valid/624548/

https://www.theguardian.com/books/2019/sep/02/why-dont-doctors-
trust-women-because-they-dont-know-much-about-us

https://time.com/4164885/daily-news-cosby-cover/

https://www.propublica.org/article/false-rape-accusations-an-
unbelievable-story

https://www.independent.co.uk/news/uk/crime/shana-grice-
murdered-stalking-fined-for-wasting-police-time-michael-lane-
trial-lewes-crown-court-east-sussex-a7637196.html

https://www.bbc.co.uk/news/uk-england-sussex-39745848

https://www.cps.gov.uk/sites/default/files/documents/publications/
perverting_course_of_justice_march_2013.pdf

https://www.theguardian.com/society/2014/jan/31/rape-claims-
police-forces-allegations

https://www.vice.com/en/article/pajqkv/rape-victims-denied-
therapy-uk-courts

https://www.theguardian.com/society/2012/jan/30/rape-victims-
acquittals-chief-prosecutor

https://www.theguardian.com/society/2021/jun/17/ministers-apologise-to-rape-victims-and-promise-reform-in-review

https://www.nytimes.com/2014/09/02/world/europe/reckoning-starts-in-britain-on-abuse-of-girls.html

https://www.bbc.co.uk/news/uk-england-london-59123551

https://www.theguardian.com/uk-news/2021/apr/30/wales-anthony-williams-who-killed-wife-will-not-have-five-year-sentence-increased

https://www.independent.co.uk/news/world/americas/brock-turner-stanford-rapist-swimmer-freed-three-months-jail-sexual-assault-a7222916.html

https://www.independent.co.uk/news/world/australasia/grace-millane-murder-trial-sex-bdsm-fetish-whiplr-new-zealand-court-a9210231.html

https://www.thejournal.ie/underwear-belfast-rape-trial-4358357-Nov2018/

https://www.independent.co.uk/news/uk/home-news/sky-news-presenter-steve-dixon-drunk-women-sex-attacks-rape-responsibility-a7536986.html

https://www.dailymail.co.uk/news/article-1270113/Youre-guilty-rape-Those-skinny-jeans-tight-remove-jury-rules.html

https://papers.ssrn.com/sol3/papers.cfm?abstract_id=2973067

Do Not Push Out Women

https://artsandculture.google.com/story/HgXhTLahLDp8Lg

https://www.parliament.uk/about/living-heritage/transformingsociety/electionsvoting/womenvote/case-studies-women-parliament/suffragettes-in-trousers/men-from-the-north/

https://users.drew.edu/~jlenz/br-liberalism-and-suffrage.html

https://www.jstor.org/stable/24529095

https://www.repository.cam.ac.uk/bitstream/handle/1810/266139/I-didn-t-know-where-to-look-formatted-for-CSH-v2.pdf

https://library.oapen.org/viewer/web/viewer.html?file=/bitstream/handle/20.500.12657/49724/9781447357971.pdf?sequence=1&isAllowed=y

https://kareningalasmith.com/2013/11/17/25th-november-whats-in-a-name/

https://www.bbc.co.uk/news/world-asia-56020674

https://www.wgtn.ac.nz/lals/resources/publications/wwp/1WWP1991v3.pdf

https://wiw-report.s3.amazonaws.com/Women_in_the_Workplace_2019.pdf

Practical Interventions

https://twitter.com/UN_Women/status/486324669369577472

https://obamawhitehouse.archives.gov/blog/2014/09/19/president-obama-launches-its-us-campaign-end-sexual-assault-campus

https://www.youtube.com/watch?v=xT2LbqtyYKQ

https://www.theguardian.com/society/2021/mar/17/the-time-for-men-to-step-up-is-right-now-what-all-men-can-do-to-help-end-violence-against-women

https://library.oapen.org/bitstream/handle/20.500.12657/49724/9781447357971.pdf?sequence=1&isAllowed=y

https://that-guy.co.uk/mean-streets-what-women-and-men-really-think-about-harassment/

https://www.bbc.co.uk/news/uk-england-57432300

https://www.theguardian.com/uk-news/2022/jan/24/met-apologises-to-academic-for-sexist-derogatory-language

https://www.theguardian.com/uk-news/2022/feb/01/met-officers-joked-raping-women-police-watchdog-racist https://www.bbc.co.uk/news/uk-england-london-58805186

Call Out Those Around You

https://banmarchive.org.uk/red-rag/
http://www.mandela.gov.za/mandela_speeches/1997/971122_
mensmarch.htm
https://journals.sagepub.com/doi/abs/10.1177/001872679905200902
http://www.alanberkowitz.com/articles/social%20norms%20
approach-short.pdf
https://www.proquest.com/openview/f252c2e8f0064718f33e4e8f968
399cc/1?pq-origsite=gscholar&cbl=7561
http://www.azrapeprevention.org/summaries_cares_2015

Don't Have All the Answers

https://www.thejournal.ie/threatening-email-katie-hannon-5657185-
Jan2022/
https://www.irishtimes.com/news/ireland/irish-news/man-exposes-
himself-during-online-vigil-for-ashling-murphy-1.4778518
https://www.gov.uk/government/news/tackling-violence-against-
women-and-girls-strategy-launched